駅弁

Recipes & stories of Japan's train bento

EKIBEN

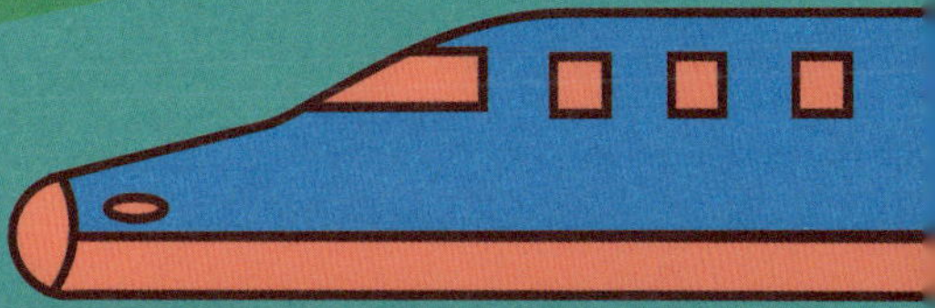

BRENDAN LIEW

Smith Street Books

CONTENTS

INTRODUCTION: PRETTY AS A PICTURE

The Shinkansen accelerates smoothly, almost imperceptibly, and the landscape begins to flow. Cities dissolve into suburbs, suburbs give way to mountains, mountains flatten into rice paddies, and finally the sea flashes into view before slipping away again. The scenery is postcard-like and fleeting, gone before you can reach for your camera.

Inside the carriage, the contrast is immediate. The Shinkansen is remarkably quiet. In an age of constant stimulation, the hush feels deliberate. Conversations are subdued, phones are silenced, and the visual noise common to public transport elsewhere is almost entirely absent. Advertising, so dominant in local subway stations, is reduced to a few discreet posters at each end of the carriage. The train feels like a refuge. While high-speed rail now exists across much of the world, travelling on a Shinkansen is an experience that remains unmistakably Japanese.

When the food cart attendant enters, she bows gently before beginning her route. The cart moves softly down the aisle, offering canned coffee, tea, soft drinks, Japanese beer, and the famously rich Hokkaido ice cream. She works with quiet precision, her movements rehearsed and purposeful. The ice cream is tempting – but you already know you have something better waiting.

Earlier, at the station, you stood before rows of neatly stacked boxes. Some were modest, wrapped simply in paper and string. Others were brightly printed with illustrations of coastlines, mountains or local mascots. Each promised something specific: a place, a flavour, a memory. After a moment's thought, you chose one, paid and slipped it into your bag. Now, as the countryside streams past the window, you lift the lid.

Inside is an ekiben.

Each grain of rice is glossy and intact. A piece of fish – salt-grilled – rests neatly beside it. There are pickles, a folded omelette, simmered vegetables, and a sweet mochi tucked into a corner. Everything is arranged with care, each element distinct, yet part of a considered whole. This is food designed to travel, but never at the expense of taste.

What you're eating is a distillation of the region you've just passed through. The rice was grown locally, nourished by the same rivers you glimpsed from the train. The fish may have come from nearby waters; the seasoning reflects local tastes, even the soy sauce is locally brewed. This sense of place is not decorative – it is fundamental, and something nowhere else can replicate.

Ekiben – short for eki bento, or 'station bento' – are meals sold at train stations and on trains across Japan. But to describe them simply as packed lunches understates their significance. Ekiben are a uniquely Japanese response to travel, geography and appetite, shaped by more than a century of movement across the country.

The first ekiben appeared in 1885 at Utsunomiya Station (100 km/60 mi north of Tokyo): a simple onigiri with a radish pickle, wrapped in bamboo bark. This unpretentious snack was a response to a government request for food to sustain travellers on the new, developing train network. From that modest beginning, an entire industry grew. Today, there are more than 2000 distinct ekiben offerings across Japan, produced by companies that often span generations. Some ekiben change with the seasons; others have remained largely untouched for decades.

The story of ekiben is inseparable from the story of train travel, and train travel is inseparable from the story of modern Japan. As railways expanded, journeys that once took days could suddenly be completed in hours; what once took hours, now takes minutes. Food needed to adapt to a new pace of life.

Ekiben makers responded with ingenuity. They learned how to prepare meals that could be eaten cold, how to balance flavours that would hold over time, and how to pack food securely without sacrificing presentation. Just as importantly, they learned how to express regional identity within the confines of a small box. Ekiben became a way to introduce travellers to local cuisine, even if they never left the train station.

Even today, in a country saturated with convenience stores and global fast-food chains, ekiben remain resiliently local. While international brands dominate much of the streetscape, the Shinkansen is one of the few places where they are notably absent. Instead, you'll find boxes celebrating regional dishes and ingredients: for example in Nagoya you will find versions of hitsumabushi and miso katsu that have been adapted for travel. In the north of the country, ekiben can feature plump seafood that has been gently braised with Hokkaido Rishiri kombu (a premium seaweed); while at the southern edge of the island of Kyushu, rich bento filled with grilled and braised wagyu and chicken can be found throughout the prefectures of Kagoshima and Miyazaki, regions that are defined by their fertile farmlands.

There is something quietly remarkable about this persistence. In a globalised world where food advertising often bears only a vague resemblance to the final product, ekiben deliver exactly what they promise. Open the lid, and the image on the box appears before you - sometimes even more carefully arranged than the photograph suggests. Vegetables look fresh, meats retain their colour, sauces stay where they should. The food inside really is as pretty as the picture.

Ekiben makers delve into regional tastes, history and ingredients in a way few other food producers do. Many draw directly from home cooking or local festival dishes. Others collaborate with established restaurants, translating their flavours into a form that can be eaten on a moving train. Some ekiben are unapologetically luxurious - there are boxes featuring Kobe wagyu beef, for example - yet even these are offered at prices far below what such ingredients would cost in a restaurant. Ekiben democratise access to regional food.

For this book, I travelled the length of Japan by Shinkansen - from the northern edge of Hokkaido to the southern reaches of Kyushu, where the tracks look out towards the East China Sea. Along the way, I encountered countless ekiben.

What struck me most was not only their quality, but the contrast between regions. Even towns that appear small or unassuming on a map possess fiercely distinct food cultures. In one city, an ekiben might celebrate scallops and oysters from cold northern waters. An hour later, the focus shifts entirely to beef and local miso, flavours that would feel out of place in the previous town. The transitions are abrupt and unapologetic.

In a world where almost everything is accessible everywhere, Japan continues to insist on regionality. This way of thinking is often compared to French wine culture, where terroir defines identity and value. Ekiben operate on the same concept. They insist that where something comes from matters - and that you can taste the difference.

This book is about more than ekiben as they are sold today. It is about the people behind them: the manufacturers who have weathered wars and economic change, and who translate local dishes into portable form; the enthusiasts who understand that packaging is communication, not decoration. It is about how food adapts to movement without losing its roots.

Ekiben also offer lessons beyond the train. The principles behind them - balance, preparation, restraint - are the same principles that make everyday cooking satisfying. Many ekiben are designed to be eaten cold or reheated, prepared in advance yet still deeply enjoyable. This practicality, refined over more than 140 years, can be used in home cooking, in a lunch bento, weeknight dinner, or for a weekend party.

The recipes that follow in this book are not exact reproductions, but interpretations — drawn from research, repeated tastings, and close observation of how each bento is composed. They aim to capture the spirit of the original: the balance of flavours, the interplay of textures, and the history that ties each element together.

Ekiben endure because they solve a problem elegantly. They feed people in motion without sacrificing quality, identity or pleasure. They remind us that even while moving quickly, we can still eat thoughtfully.

So let's go on a journey together - across platforms and prefectures, through rice fields and travelling beside coastlines, opening boxes along the way. Inside each one is more than a meal. It is a place, a moment, and a story waiting to be tasted.

How to use this book

In this book, we'll explore more than 30 ekiben, travelling from snowy Hokkaido in the north to temperate Kyushu in the south. While I've tried to present a wide range of styles, there are dozens more ekiben I would have loved to include. The bentos featured here are not a definitive list of the 'best' ekiben, but rather a representative taste of what's on offer. There are simply too many great ekiben.

For each ekiben, we'll look at its history, its contents and what makes it special, before offering recipes you can recreate at home. These are not official recipes from the manufacturers, but thoughtful approximations based on tasting, research and ingredients available outside Japan.

Some ekiben in this book are not accompanied by recipes. In some cases, the ingredients are difficult to source outside Japan - such as anago (saltwater conger eel) - while others rely on produce that is prohibitively expensive, like Tottori snow crab. Certain preparations are also highly specialised, requiring techniques that are impractical in a home kitchen, such as the precise methods behind Osaka's hakozushi (page 148) or Toyama's Masu No Sushi (page 92).

These dishes are included not as instructions to replicate, but as part of a broader portrait of ekiben culture - an invitation to encounter them as part of your journey, as they are meant to be experienced.

Use this book to relive favourite Shinkansen memories, to explore local foods from places you'd like to visit, or simply as inspiration for your next work lunch or weeknight dinner.

EKIBEN: A BRIEF HISTORY

When Japan's railways were still new, no one could yet predict what train travel would become. The country's first railway opened on 14 October 1872, connecting Shimbashi in Tokyo with Yokohama, but the story of ekiben begins a little later.

In 1885, when the Japanese Railway – now part of the JR Tohoku Main Line – opened between Ueno (in northeast Tokyo) and Utsunomiya (100 km/60 mi north of Tokyo), the government hoped to provide passengers with something to eat during their journey. Restaurants, however, were hesitant. Rail travel was still an experiment, passenger numbers were uncertain, and few businesses were willing to prepare food for travellers who might never arrive.

Shiragiya, a local ryokan, did take the risk though. It offered travellers a modest meal: two sesame-coated onigiri, a small portion of pickled daikon, all wrapped in bamboo bark. It cost 5 sen – roughly the equivalent of 100 yen today. Simple, portable and practical, this unassuming bundle is widely regarded as the first ekiben.

At the time, it was not a 'bento' in the way we understand it now. There was no sense of regional identity or presentation. It was sustenance, nothing more. But it planted a seed.

As railway construction accelerated, that seed found fertile ground. In 1889, the Tokaido Main Line connecting Tokyo and Kobe was completed, creating a vital artery through the heart of Japan. Travel times reduced from over 20 hours to approximately 15 hours, making trips more attractive. Passenger numbers increased, and the act of eating while travelling began to feel like a natural extension of the journey itself. Ekiben became companions on the journey, their labels doubling as guides to local sights and small souvenirs to take home.

That same year, at Himeji Station, Maneki Foods introduced a new kind of railway meal: the makunouchi bento (see page 12). Unlike the earlier onigiri, this was a composed meal, filled with white rice and what were traditionally considered the 'three sacred treasures' of Japanese food – fish, kamaboko (pink-ringed fish cake) and dashimaki tamago (rolled omelette, page 26) – alongside simmered dishes and pickles. It was generous, carefully arranged and satisfying. This style would become the prototype for the makunouchi ekiben still found across Japan today.

As railways spread, so did ekiben. Each new line brought new stations, and each station presented an opportunity. Japan's geography played a crucial role in shaping what followed. Stretching from north to south, with sharply defined seasons and access to both mountain and sea, the country offered an extraordinary range of ingredients. Ekiben makers, usually small local restaurants or inns, drew from their experience and surroundings to create meals that reflected local flavours.

Ekiben became a form of welcome. To open a bento was to be introduced to a place – its produce, techniques and preferences. A journey across Japan could be tasted station by station.

Credit: The Railway Museum

1. *Station stand sales in 1955.*

Credit: The Railway Museum

Credit: The Railway Museum

3. *Standing sales at the station (Kuriyama Station on the Muroran Main Line, 1963).*

2. *A Joto O-bento, or first-class bento, sold at Abiko Station in Chiba Prefecture in 1919.*

Rather than listing dishes, this label presents a stylised route map of the Joban Line, marking stations, bridges, and well-known scenic spots for travellers. The bento is a companion to the journey itself, reflecting an era when ekiben packaging functioned as both meal and travel guide.

Early trains stopped for long stretches of time, sometimes for several minutes. This allowed another ekiben tradition to take hold: platform sales. Vendors called out to passengers, bento boxes stacked on wooden trays, selling directly through open carriage windows. These scenes – now iconic – cemented ekiben as an essential part of railway culture and helped expand their reach.

As Japan entered the 20th century, ekiben evolved alongside the nation itself. From the late Taisho period (roughly 1920–1926) through to the end of the Second World War, ekiben took on a new role. Demand for food increased dramatically, particularly near military facilities and transportation hubs. Ekiben were called upon to feed soldiers in large numbers, giving rise to what were known as gunben, or military bento.

This period marked a turning point. Ekiben production shifted from small-scale preparation to mass production. Efficiency became as important as flavour. While this era placed enormous strain on makers, it also laid the groundwork for the logistical systems that would later support the industry's growth.

After the war, Japan rebuilt with astonishing speed. The period of rapid economic growth that followed brought with it a leisure boom. Travel was no longer limited to necessity; people travelled for pleasure, for sightseeing, for family trips. Rail passenger numbers surged, and with them, demand for ekiben.

Many of the ekiben now considered classics were born during this time. In 1954, Kiyoken introduced its Shumai Bento (page 110) in Yokohama. In 1958, Oginoya released Toge no Kamameshi at Yokokawa Station. Both are still sold today, unchanged in spirit, and deeply associated with their regions.

Yet progress carried consequences. Faster trains meant fewer and shorter station stops. The expansion of expressways and the rise of private car ownership reduced reliance on rail. Gradually, the environment that had allowed ekiben to flourish began to transform.

By 1967, membership in the Central Association of Ekiben Producers peaked at 405 companies. From there, numbers steadily declined. Some makers withdrew from the business, others closed entirely.

Makunouchi: A meal between moments

The term makunouchi comes from the world of traditional Japanese theatre.

Maku means 'curtain', and *nouchi* means 'inside' or 'between'. Together, '*makunouchi*' refers to the intermission between acts, when the stage curtain was closed.

During these breaks, audiences – and sometimes performers – would eat a well-balanced meal. The food needed to be compact, neat, and easy to eat without disrupting the performance, not too heavy or cumbersome. Over time, the style of food eaten 'during the curtain break' came to be known as makunouchi.

When rail travel expanded in the late 19th century, early ekiben makers adopted this familiar format. A makunouchi bento typically featured white rice with a variety of small dishes such as fish, tamagoyaki, kamaboko and simmered vegetables.

So, while makunouchi bento are now synonymous with trains and travel, their name and structure trace back to the rhythm of the theatre – a meal designed for the space between moments, rather than the main event itself.

It was a difficult period, one that forced the industry to rethink its future.

What followed was not retreat, but adaptation and consolidation.

Ekiben makers across Japan began experimenting, responding creatively to changing conditions. A significant innovation came in 1987, when Awajiya introduced the Atchichi Steam Bento. Using a self-heating container, this ekiben challenged one of the industry's long-held principles – that ekiben must be delicious even when cold. Suddenly, warmth was possible. The heated container quickly spread nationwide and remains a familiar feature today.

The following year, in 1988, the Central Association established the Ekiben Mark. Featuring a square bento divided by wooden partitions and centred around the Hinomaru (the red sun disc on the Japanese flag), the mark symbolised harmony, tradition and national identity. This mark, displayed on the ekiben packaging of the association's members, served as both a guarantee of authenticity, and an assertion that ekiben were more than convenience food – they were cultural artefacts.

The early 2000s brought new challenges. The rise of large 'eki-naka' ('inside the station' shopping and dining complexes) offered travellers an unprecedented range of dining options. For ekiben, competition intensified. Choice expanded, attention fragmented.

Then, in 2013, something shifted. Washoku – traditional Japanese cuisine – was registered as a UNESCO Intangible Cultural Heritage. With this recognition came renewed interest, both within Japan and abroad, in foods that expressed regional identity and tradition. Ekiben, long tied to place and journey, found themselves newly relevant.

Department store ekiben fairs grew in popularity. Major terminal stations opened dedicated ekiben shops selling products from across the country. Inbound tourism increased, and with it, curiosity about regional railway food. Ekiben sales stabilised, even strengthened.

Then came COVID-19.

From early 2020, the pandemic disrupted daily life on an unprecedented scale. Travel was discouraged. Crowds were avoided. Eating on trains all but disappeared. For an industry inseparable from movement, tourism and shared space, the impact was severe.

Yet once again, ekiben makers adapted. Frozen ekiben were developed for home consumption. Mail-order collaborations connected producers across regions. Drive-through sales appeared where possible. Ekiben vending machines became common.

Late 2022 marked the 150th anniversary of the opening of Japan's railways. To commemorate the occasion, 31 companies released reprint ekiben labels inspired by historical designs. Each included a miniature clear file featuring a Meiji-era railway print. The project united makers under a shared theme and demonstrated, once again, the collective strength of ekiben culture.

As I write this book in 2026, it's been 141 years since that first simple bundle of onigiri was sold on a station platform. Across wars, economic upheavals, technological change and a global pandemic, ekiben have endured. Many producers have been in business for over a century, carrying forward skills and recipes, along with local pride.

Ekiben are not static, and never have been. They respond to place, to movement, to the world around them. As trains carry people towards new destinations, ekiben remain what they have always been: small companions on the journey, or fond reminders of places already passed.

INTERVIEW WITH
KENICHI FUKUOKA

'The custom of collecting and taking home ekiben wrapping paper, or kakeshi, has been around for over a hundred years, and I believe this is also one way to create travel memories.'

EKIBEN OBSESSIVES

Kenichi Fukuoka is the founder of Ekiben Museum (ekibenmuseum.org/ekiben). His website has catalogued over 11,000 ekiben since 2001. He personally manages the website and has tried more than 9000 ekiben since the website's inception.

Q: *PLEASE TELL ME HOW YOU BECAME INTERESTED IN EKIBEN.*

A:

As a student, I loved travelling and trains, and I would travel all over Japan using a student rail pass. I learned that ekiben were sold at train stations, and that some had become local specialties, but they were too expensive for a student, so I couldn't afford to buy many. I bought and ate the Masu No Sushi (page 92) from Toyama Station, and it was so delicious that I would buy it every time I went there. It remains a famous ekiben in Japan.

In the '90s, as the internet became more widespread, creating websites became popular in Japan. I created and deleted websites for travel, railways and other topics. In 1999, a website I created that featured train timetables became a hit, and in 2001, I began posting introductions to ekiben as well, which also became a hit. I started collecting ekiben to post on the site, and I was impressed by their individuality and diversity. To this day, I personally run the Ekiben Museum website.

Q: *WHAT MAKES EKIBEN SO SPECIAL FOR YOU?*

A:

Whether they have ekiben or not, I enjoy going to places I've never been, seeing scenery I've never seen before, and eating foods I've never tried before. I believe that ekiben can become part of travel memories, not only for their contents but also for their appearance, the design of the outer box and wrapping paper. The custom of collecting and taking home ekiben wrapping paper, or kakeshi, has been around for over a hundred years, and I believe this is also one way to create travel memories.

Thirty-five years ago, I got off an overnight train from Ueno Station at Morioka Station, and took a Yamada Line train to Miyako Station at 9 am. I remember eating a delicious salmon and salmon roe ekiben. I couldn't remember the name of the bento, but I happened to come across a Sakekko Chirashi revival sold at a department store's ekiben convention in 2008, and it brought back memories.

Q: *WHAT'S YOUR IDEAL EKIBEN?*

A:

The classic ideal of an ekiben is a meal prepared near the station and sold directly on the platform. Today, such ekiben are increasingly rare.

From the beginning, ekiben were designed as pre-made meals that could be eaten later on a train, which meant they needed to taste good even when cold. This requirement shaped their texture and flavour. Ingredients that spoil easily are avoided, rice is slightly firm with little moisture, and flavours are often a little stronger so they remain satisfying after time has passed. The ingredients are also arranged carefully so that the contents hold their shape and do not become disordered during travel.

Today, many ekiben are produced in kitchens or factories outside the station and transported by truck to be sold at stations or commercial facilities. In that sense, their production is not so different from other prepared foods.

Yet regardless of where they are made, certain qualities still define an ekiben: the box, container and decorative wrapping paper (known as kakeshi) often carry distinctive designs, while the contents reflect the character of a particular region or the identity of the shop that produces it. Together these elements give an ekiben its unique sense of place. For example, Yokohama Station's Shumai Bento (page 110) has a yellow kakeshi placed on a wooden container, tied crosswise with string, and cylindrical-shaped white rice accompanied by five shumai and other side dishes. All of the ingredients are unique to the ekiben shop, Kiyoken, and retain a strong resemblance to ekiben from over half a century ago.

The aforementioned Masu No Sushi from Toyama Station was a local Toyama dish from over 100 years ago before it was turned into an ekiben. Its popularity as an ekiben has made masu sushi a Toyama specialty.

Q: *HOW HAVE YOU SEEN EKIBEN EVOLVE OVER THE YEARS?*

A:

Ekiben peaked in the 1970s, but have been declining ever since. This is due to the decline of railways due to the spread of automobiles and aeroplanes (since the 1970s); the shortening of travel times and the decline in food demand due to faster train speeds (since the 1970s); the spread of takeaway bento shops and convenience stores (since the 1980s); the increase in station shops due to the dismantling and privatisation of the national railways (since the 1980s); the increase in station shops due to the conversion of stations into commercial facilities (since the 2000s); the closure of ekiben shops due to improvements to railways and urban areas in front of stations (since the 2000s); and the financial difficulties and lack of successors for ekiben shops (since the 2000s).

It's said that the number of ekiben shops has fallen by 80 per cent since its peak, but the number of ekiben boxes has doubled since its peak. This is because the ekiben shops' offerings have increased. New bento boxes are released almost every month, and during the cold winter months department stores hold large-scale ekiben sales events called ekiben taiko (ekiben conventions).

Larger stations like Tokyo, Shin-Osaka and Hakata offer ekiben year-round at ekiben shops comparable in scale to ekiben taiko. Tokyo Station's ekiben shop, Ekiben Matsuri (page 74), is open from 5 am until late at night, and apparently sells about 20,000 ekiben per day.

It's clear that ekiben, as a type of bento, is here to stay. The word 'ekiben' appears in any commercially available Japanese dictionary. Railway operators such as JR East and JR Kyushu are holding ekiben events such as fairs and competitions. I don't think we'll ever see an era in which railways again become the king of transportation or ekiben become the main food source, but I think ekiben will survive.

Q: *WHAT ARE SOME OF THE MOST MEMORABLE EKIBEN YOU'VE HAD?*

A:

There have been many, but one example is Niigata Station's Ebi Senryo Chirashi (page 88). Originally created by a luxury travel brand, I was impressed by its postcard-worthy outer box and the many ingredients hidden by the thick, golden omelette. I was surprised by its sudden popularity seven years after its release in 2002.

Otaru Station's Umi no Kagayaki (Sea Shine) and Yonago Station's Umi no Treasure Chest (Sea Treasure Box) also feature beautiful seafood chirashi sushi. The Katsuo Tataki Bento is packed with bonito and ice packs at the time of purchase, making it the one and only ekiben featuring raw fish, and it has been around for 35 years.

Tobu Nikko Station's Nikko Buried Treasure Bento was sold by reservation from 2006 to 2024, and was the most expensive ekiben in the country, costing 150,000–237,000 yen. The floral-patterned furoshiki wrapping cloth, the beautiful Nikko-bori wooden container (a Nikko specialty), and the luxurious and beautiful contents that included wagyu beef, crab, and trout sushi, all made this an exceptional ekiben – truly beautiful in every respect.

Q: *DO YOU HAVE ANY ADVICE FOR FIRST-TIME EKIBEN BUYERS?*

A:

If you go to a station kiosk that sells ekiben and choose an ekiben that's popular, one with the most stock, or one you've already heard of, it will be a good ekiben. If you keep trying ekiben after that, you'll start to enjoy new ekiben and appreciate the hits and misses.

Ekiben are sold during the day, so unless you're at a major station, they may be out of stock or unavailable in the morning or evening. I recommend buying ekiben between 10 and 11 am and 2 and 3 pm. Many ekiben will last until the evening.

¥150.
日本食堂（株）謹製
今は遠き
明治十八年。
の新製品〈駅
塩にぎりめし
香の物。竹の
てつまるる。あ
意
也。
㈱日本食堂 調理所 謹製
¥400
¥400
北海道の味
ほたてご飯
特製
お早めにお召し上り下さい。
日本食堂㈱
函館列車営業所
北海道函館市大手町6番19号
御弁当
日本食堂
調整
¥500

BUILDING AN EKIBEN

Ekiben vs bento: what's the difference?

Traditionally, ekiben were sold only at train stations, which places a number of constraints on their design:

- they must be safe to eat unrefrigerated for extended periods
- they assume no access to heating – no ovens or microwaves
- they must withstand transport, movement and vibration without spilling or shifting.

As a result, ekiben are tightly packed, rely primarily on cooked or preserved ingredients, and are designed to be enjoyed fully at room temperature.

Ekiben boxes are disposable and lightweight. Unlike bentos taken to work, they are not usually refrigerated or microwaved before being eaten – though you don't need to follow this rule. The idea underpinning this book is to take ekiben recipes and apply them to your everyday life.

How to construct your ekiben

Ekiben are usually – though not always – composed of rice, protein and vegetables. This book explores a number of Japan's most popular ekiben, and provides recipes to cook most of the elements that are included in these delicious packaged meals.

You can decide whether you want to follow the recipes to recreate these ekiben in your own home, or alternatively you can pick and choose elements from across the ekiben to make your own unique ekiben.

If you choose to build your own boxed meal, here are a few guiding principles to creating satisfying and well-balanced bentos which I have learned through research and observation.

1. Base

RICE

Japan is a country of rice, and most ekiben use cooked rice as their foundation. Fill your bento box to a depth of around 1–1.5 cm (½ in) with rice. This allows toppings to flavour the rice evenly, keeping the base and toppings in balance. In this book, we use Japanese table rice for its neutral flavour, gentle sweetness, and ability to stay moist while retaining distinct grains.

This rice layer typically makes up about 50 per cent of the bento.

TAKIKOMI GOHAN / GOMOKU GOHAN

Takikomi gohan is rice that is cooked with ingredients in seasoned stock rather than water. Gomoku gohan is a variation that traditionally includes five ingredients in addition to rice.

NOODLES

The most common noodle base for bento is yakisoba – wheat noodles stir-fried with vegetables, meat and seafood in a sweet-savoury sauce similar to Worcestershire sauce. In Nagasaki, I encountered sara udon (page 210) – crisp fried noodles that stayed crunchy even after cooling. Noodles should generally be fried to prevent clumping. Boiled, starchy noodles like udon tend to stick together when cold, while soba noodles work better due to their lower gluten content.

KETCHUP RICE OR SPAGHETTI NAPOLITAN

For Western-style bentos with richer proteins – such as those with hamburg steak (page 50) or fried chicken (page 96) – the acidity and umami of ketchup rice or spaghetti napolitan makes a perfect base. Ketchup rice or spaghetti napolitan can also stand alone as the primary bento filling, without being topped with other ingredients.

2. Protein

Common ekiben proteins include meat, fish, eggs and tofu. As with commercially prepared ekiben, everything should be thoroughly cooked to ensure food safety during transport and storage.

Proteins should be tender, juicy and well seasoned – and, unless they are soft and easy to slice (as in the case of hamburg), they should be cut into bite-sized pieces for ease of eating, whether on a train, park bench or in the lunchroom. While this book provides many examples of popular proteins, experimentation is encouraged.

3. Vegetables

Vegetables most often appear in ekiben in the form of pickles. Even fried foods lose their crispness after packing and storing, so pickles provide a crunchy element that's difficult to preserve in other foods. They also add colour and contrast, and introduce acidity that refreshes the palate. Japan has an enormous range of pickled vegetables; feel free to make your own or use good-quality packaged varieties.

Another common preparation is ohitashi (page 28) – blanched vegetables marinated in dashi, which offers more flavour than plain blanched greens, while still remaining clean and restrained.

2.
3.
1.
4.
1.
5.

Ekiben equipment

Ekiben can be made with minimal equipment, but a few tools help achieve a professional result.

1. Presentation box

One of the most overlooked parts of ekiben is the right container. Ekiben boxes are generally flatter than typical takeaway containers, allowing ingredients to be packed tightly so they don't shift during transport. While it is important the container is watertight, ekiben are made with little excess liquid, and the rice base usually absorbs excess moisture.

Historically, ekiben containers were made from bamboo, wood or paper – lightweight, inexpensive materials ideal for carrying while squeezing onto a busy train.

2. Rice cooker

Most ekiben use rice as the base, so having a good-quality electric rice cooker, although not essential, will save a lot of time and stress, as they ensure your rice cooks evenly. (With cheaper rice cookers, rice tends to stick to the bottom and burn, resulting in wastage.)

A non-stick rice cooker is also much easier to clean. Some ekiben, such as Ujiie Kaki Meshi (page 38) and Hotate Meshi (page 44), include takikomi gohan (rice cooked with ingredients in seasoned stock). This rice tends to contain some sugar (in the form of mirin), that can stick to the bottom of a pot, but this is much less likely when using a non-stick rice cooker.

Another option is a donabe (pictured), or traditional claypot, for cooking rice. Although they aren't the one button solution electric rice cookers are, they provide even heat retention and the double lid design seals in moisture and increases pressure, resulting in sweeter, more evenly cooked rice.

3. Rice moulds

How the rice is shaped changes how a bento is eaten. Small cylinders, known as tawara gata gohan, as seen in the Shumai Bento (page 110), are easy to pick up and work well when components are eaten separately. Onigiri, meanwhile, guide the eater towards specific flavour combinations by filling or mixing ingredients into the rice.

In the Musubi Maru Bento (page 60), rice appears both as a base and as onigiri. The salmon sitting atop rice means it should be eaten together, while the onigiri is enjoyed simply with nori, highlighting the rice itself.

4. Patty pans

Disposable or reusable patty pans (or cupcake liners) are useful for holding pickles or salads, preventing dressings from affecting the taste of other ekiben components. Plastic, silicone or paper versions all work well.

5. Kushi / skewers

Short skewers can group ingredients meant to be eaten together – such as duck and chestnut – or make items like fried chicken easier to pick up. They can also be used as an additional utensil for dessert, to avoid transferring savoury flavours to your sweet mochi.

BASIC RECIPES

RICE

米

Rice is the foundation of most bento, and choosing good-quality Japanese rice makes a noticeable difference. It stays soft and moist when cold, unlike long-grain varieties that harden and become gritty.

Serves 2

200 g (7 oz) short-grain white rice (see Notes)
250–375 ml (1–1½ cups) water (see Notes)

To wash the rice, fill a large bowl with water, place the rice in a sieve and immerse the sieve in the water. Move the grains back and forth inside the sieve to release the excess starch from the rice. Drain the water and wash the rice another two times, or until the water is clear. Drain the rice well.

If using a donabe or lidded saucepan, place the rice and water in the vessel. Allow to soak for 15 minutes. Turn the heat to high and bring to the boil uncovered. When the water is boiling, stir the rice once, then cover with an airtight lid and turn the heat down to very low.

Allow to cook for 14 minutes. Switch the heat off and rest, covered, for a further 14 minutes.

After this time has elapsed, the rice is ready.

If using a rice cooker, add the washed rice to the rice cooker along with the water. Top up with additional water if needed to reach the liquid level recommended by the rice cooker manufacturer. Cook according to the rice cooker instructions.

NOTES //

While many ekiben use hyper-local rice varieties, choosing Japanese rice from regions such as Niigata, Hokkaido, Akita and Aomori will yield excellent results.

The ratio of rice to water depends on the rice being used. Generally, the fresher or better quality the rice, the closer the ratio is to 1:1. The ratio used here will generally work for most rice, but judge for yourself whether you need more water because your rice is dry, or less if the rice is too damp after cooking.

The resting time is extremely important for rice cooked in saucepans or traditional donabe. If the rice isn't adequately rested, much of it will remain stuck to the bottom of the cooking vessel. Additional resting time, especially in a donabe that holds its heat well, is not a problem.

This recipe makes enough for two people. You can easily scale up the quantities to serve more people – the method and cooking time will remain the same.

DASHI

出汁

Dashi, a clear broth made from kombu and katsuobushi, is the foundation of Japanese cooking. It's used to cook rice, vegetables, seafood and soups.

On this page are three methods for making it at home. The second method, which uses dashi tea bags, offers the best balance of flavour, cost and convenience. Many instant dashi packs include dried mackerel or sardine, adding complexity compared to bonito alone.

METHOD 1: THE TRADITIONAL WAY

Makes 2 litres (2 qts)

5 cm (2 in) piece kombu (approx. 12 g/ ½ oz)
2 litres (2 qts) filtered water, at room temperature
25 g (1 cup, loosely packed) katsuobushi (dried bonito flakes)

Add the kombu and water to a large saucepan, then allow to steep for at least 30 minutes at room temperature, or up to 8 hours or overnight in the fridge.

Place the pan over high heat. When bubbles start rising in the pan (at about 70°C/160°F), remove the kombu.

Bring the water to 80°C (175°F), then add the katsuobushi. When small bubbles start rising again (at about 85°C/185°F), turn off the heat.

When the katsuobushi sinks to the bottom of the pan, strain the broth through a fine-mesh sieve or muslin cloth. Do not press the katsuobushi, as this will introduce unwanted flavours.

Allow the dashi to cool, then refrigerate for up to 3 days.

You can use the left-over kombu and katsuobushi to make niban dashi ('second dashi') by re-simmering the ingredients for 10 minutes. The strained niban dashi makes a good base for a stew.

METHOD 2: THE QUICK WAY

Makes 750 ml (3 cups)

750 ml (3 cups) water
1 instant dashi tea bag

Bring the water to a simmer in a small saucepan, then add the dashi tea bag. Press the tea bag down into the water and simmer for 2 minutes.

Switch the heat off and taste the broth. If it's not strong enough, you can leave the dashi bag in for another 1–5 minutes.

When the broth is flavourful, remove the dashi bag and allow the liquid to cool if not using immediately. It will keep for 2 days in the fridge.

METHOD 3: THE INSTANT WAY

Makes 750 ml (3 cups)

750 ml (3 cups) boiling water
1 tablespoon instant dashi powder (such as Hondashi)

Whisk together the boiling water and dashi powder.

Taste and add more water or powder until you have a balanced dashi.

This dashi is best used immediately.

GYOKU

EGG・玉

This slow-baked, custard-like omelette has subtle sweetness and a savoury depth from the seafood, which also adds a subtle richness rather than fishiness to the egg.

This recipe uses an 18 cm (7 in) square ovenproof tamago pan, although you could use a square baking tray instead.

Makes 24 pieces

8 eggs
100 g (3½ oz) caster (superfine) sugar
2 tablespoons mirin
2 tablespoons sake
2 tablespoons honey
150 g (5½ oz) yama imo paste (see Note)
100 g (3½ oz) white fish meat or hanpen
40 g (1½ oz) scallop, without roe
120 g (4½ oz) prawn (shrimp) meat

Preheat the oven to 130°C (265°F).

Grease your tamagoyaki pan with oil and line with baking paper (for easier removal of the omelette).

Place all the ingredients in a blender and blend until smooth.

Pass the mixture through a fine-mesh sieve to remove any large particles.

Place your tamago pan over low heat. To test the pan is hot enough, flick a bead of water onto the pan, if it sizzles for a few seconds before evaporating you can move to the next step.

Pour in the batter and tap the pan on your work surface a couple of times to remove any large air bubbles.

Transfer to the oven and bake the omelette for 30 minutes, or until the top is set.

Remove from the oven and place a sheet of baking paper over the pan, cutting it to the size of the omelette.

Immediately place a board over the top and flip to transfer the omelette from the pan onto the board.

Slide the omelette back into the pan and remove the baking paper on top of the omelette. Return to the oven for another 30 minutes to cook the other side.

Remove the omelette from the pan and allow to cool. Once fully cooled, it will keep refrigerated in an airtight container for up to 5 days.

When serving, cut the omelette into four lengths, then cut each length into six portions, to yield 24 pieces in total.

NOTE //

Yama imo (Japanese mountain potato) has a sticky texture like okra. When fresh, it's crunchy, but outside Japan it's usually sold as a sticky paste that can be mixed into savoury recipes such as gyoku or tsukune (page 106). It can also be served over rice.

1.
Gyoku
(page 24)
2.
Dashimaki
tamago
(page 26)
3.
Kinshi tamago
(page 27)

DASHIMAKI TAMAGO

DASHI ROLLED OMELETTE・だし巻き卵

A soft, rolled omelette central to Japanese home cooking. The technique takes practice, but even imperfect rolls are delicious! A 20 cm (8 in) square non-stick tamagoyaki pan is strongly recommended.

Makes 1 rolled omelette

4 eggs
120 ml (4 fl oz) dashi (page 23)
1 teaspoon soy sauce
2 teaspoons mirin
a pinch of salt
1 teaspoon potato starch
2 tablespoons neutral oil

In a bowl, whisk together the eggs, dashi, soy sauce, mirin and salt.

Place the potato starch in a separate bowl. Strain a little of the egg mixture – about 60 ml (¼ cup) – into the bowl and whisk it into the potato starch until combined. Strain in the remaining egg mixture and whisk until smooth and no streaks of egg yolk or white are visible.

Heat your pan over medium heat and add the oil. Swirl the oil around to coat the pan, then pour the oil into a small bowl and reserve.

Drop a little egg mixture into the pan. The mix should bubble and set in about 5–10 seconds. If it sets faster than this, the pan is too hot. Remove from the heat to cool slightly. If it takes longer, increase the heat slightly and retest.

Pour one-third of the egg mixture into the pan and swirl to evenly coat the pan. Using chopsticks, puncture any large air bubbles to create a mostly flat surface.

When the egg mixture is mostly set, begin rolling the egg over, starting from the side furthest away from you and rolling towards you. You should have a squarish jelly roll–shaped omelette.

Using chopsticks, dip a piece of paper towel into the reserved oil and use that to grease the empty side of the pan. Push the omelette to the side of the pan furthest from you and grease where the omelette previously was.

Pour in another one-third of the egg mixture and swirl around the pan, lifting the omelette so the raw egg goes underneath and sticks the new egg with the omelette. This also prevents the omelette getting too browned on the bottom.

When the egg is mostly set, repeat the rolling process and complete the omelette with the remaining egg mixture. Turn the omelette out onto a cutting board, then carefully slice while still hot. Transfer to a serving dish, or allow to cool and chill. Use within 2 days.

KINSHI TAMAGO

GOLD THREAD EGG・錦糸卵

Serves 4

6 eggs
2 tablespoons mirin
1 teaspoon caster (superfine) sugar
1 teaspoon salt
2 tablespoons neutral oil

Literally translated as 'gold thread egg', kinshi tamago is a thin, sweet omelette that is sliced into fine strands and used to cover rice in bento or chirashi sushi ('scattered sushi'), providing extra protein and flavour to the rice base. You can make a large batch and freeze it, then slice (while still frozen) only what you need for each day.

A tamagoyaki (or 'tamago') pan is a special square pan that is mostly used for making rolled omelettes (dashimaki tamago; see opposite).

In a bowl, whisk together the eggs, mirin, sugar and salt, using a hand whisk or stick blender. Strain through a fine-mesh sieve to remove any large particles.

Heat a non-stick pan or tamagoyaki pan over medium heat and add the oil. Swirl the oil around to coat the pan, then pour the oil into a small bowl and reserve.

Drop a little egg mixture into the pan. The mix should bubble and set in about 5–10 seconds. If it sets faster than this, the pan is too hot. Remove from the heat to cool slightly. If it takes longer, increase the heat slightly and retest.

Pour in only enough egg to thinly cover the surface of the pan, swirling to cover the whole base evenly. Cook for about 30 seconds to 1 minute, until set.

Flip the omelette over and cook for a further 10 seconds, then remove from the pan – the egg should still be beautifully golden, not browned.

Leave to cool and repeat with the remaining egg mixture, wiping out the pan each time and greasing the pan with some of the reserved oil.

Once the egg has cooled completely, wrap and freeze until required. The frozen egg will keep for up to 1 month.

To use, slice the omelette very finely and spread over rice.

OHITASHI

BLANCHED VEGETABLES・おひたし

Ohitashi is a clean, versatile vegetable preparation ideal for bento. Unlike a salad, it won't discolour and doesn't need to be dressed before eating.

In this recipe I call for spinach or shimeji mushrooms, but feel free to experiment with many different vegetables (or a combination of vegetables, if you prefer). Simply adjust the blanching time as necessary.

Serves 4

200 g (7 oz) spinach or shimeji mushrooms
500 ml (2 cups) dashi (page 23), cold
60 ml (¼ cup) mirin
60 ml (¼ cup) soy sauce

Bring a saucepan of water to the boil and prepare a bowl of iced water.

Blanch the vegetables in the boiling water for 1–2 minutes, until cooked. Transfer to the iced water until fully cooled.

Mix together the dashi, mirin and soy sauce and divide into two even portions.

Squeeze the water from the vegetables and place the vegetables in half the dashi mixture for 30 minutes.

Drain and discard the first dashi mix, then place the vegetables in the second dashi mixture and soak again for at least 30 minutes, until required. This step increases the flavour of the vegetables, as the first marinade will become watery and less flavoursome over time.

The vegetables can be refrigerated in the mixture for up to 2 days.

NIMONO

BRAISED VEGETABLES・煮物

Serves 4

1 daikon, about 400–500 g (14 oz–1 lb 2 oz), peeled and cut into 2 cm (¾ in) thick rounds
55 g (¼ cup) short-grain white rice (see Note)
800 ml (27 fl oz) dashi (page 23)
60 ml (¼ cup) soy sauce
3 tablespoons caster (superfine) sugar
2 tablespoons sake
1 tablespoon mirin
300 g (10½ oz) block fried tofu, cut into bite-sized pieces

Braised vegetables are the cornerstone of so many bento. Whether it's a braised shiitake mushroom to anchor a beef dish, or a carrot cut to look like a flower, sitting on a 'field' of kinshi tamago (page 27), braised vegetables are everywhere. This recipe sits alongside ohitashi (opposite), because where ohitashi is good for delicate vegetables and leafy greens, nimono works best for hard or dried vegetables such as carrot, pumpkin, potato, lotus root and bamboo shoots. Koya tofu, a freeze-dried tofu, can also be rehydrated in this broth, and will absorb all the flavour from the dashi and vegetables.

This version uses daikon and atsuage tofu (deep-fried tofu), but vegetable substitutions from the list above are encouraged.

Place the daikon and rice in a saucepan, pour in enough water to cover the daikon and bring to the boil.

Allow to boil for 20 minutes, or until the daikon is almost cooked; a knife should slip through easily.

Drain the daikon and discard the liquid and rice; this will help remove any bitterness from the daikon.

In a clean saucepan, combine the dashi, soy sauce, sugar, sake and mirin. Add the daikon and tofu.

Cover with a cartouche (a round of baking paper with a small hole cut in the centre) and bring to a simmer over low heat. Simmer for about 30 minutes, until the daikon has taken on the flavour of the broth.

Remove from the heat and leave to cool in the broth. The vegetables will keep in the fridge for up to 3 days.

NOTE //

Boiling daikon with rice helps to remove excess bitterness. This step is unique to cooking daikon in this style, so there is no need to add rice if you are preparing other vegetables in this style.

TSUKEMONO

PICKLES・漬物

Pickles are an essential part of ekiben. As flavours mellow during travel and foods that were once crisp soften after packing, tsukemono restore vitality. They bring back contrast – crunch, brightness, bursts of acidity and salt – along with welcome flashes of colour that elevate the entire box.

You can buy ready-made pickles, or prepare your own at home. Both have their place, and many excellent ekiben rely on simple, familiar pickle varieties.

All of the pickles on this page are easily store-bought.

GARI

Thinly sliced ginger pickled in sweet vinegar; clean and refreshing

BENISHOGA

Julienned ginger pickled in umeboshi vinegar; crunchy and sharply tangy

TAKUAN

Sun-dried daikon pickled in rice bran; very crisp, with a vivid yellow colour. Takuan pairs well with almost any ekiben, despite its famously assertive aroma.

TAKANAZUKE

Salt-cured Japanese mustard greens, chopped and sometimes flavoured with chilli or mustard

Recipes for **amazu-zuke** (sweet vinegar pickles, page 197), **asazuke** (light pickles, page 221) and **shoyuzuke** (soy-based pickles, page 164) appear throughout the book, offering simple ways to add contrast and character to your own bentos.

SEA & SNOW

NORTHERN JAPAN

·

Hokkaido & Tohoku

Snow gathers along platform edges, the sea darkens and distances feel longer than the map suggests. Trains are infrequent here, their pace unhurried compared to the rush further south. Food, too, is shaped by cold and patience. In places where winter closes roads and storms roughen the coast, meals are built to last – salted, cured, braised, packed with care. Everything simmered slowly together as takikomi gohan, a harmonious blend of land and sea.

Rice fields stretch towards the horizon, yielding sweet, resilient grains that anchor seafood drawn from cold waters: oysters, scallops, salmon, squid. Nothing is rushed. Life moves in step with the seasons, at the mercy of the weather and the tides, taking only what nature provides. In these regions, preservation is not a nostalgic practice but a necessity – a quiet dialogue with climate that still defines the cuisine today.

As the train moves south through Iwate and Yamagata, mountains replace open sea. Valleys narrow, towns gather along rivers, and the food turns inward. You begin to taste the land as much as the water: miso deepened by long winters, wild vegetables harvested at the edge of snowmelt, meat gradually claiming a larger place at the table. This is food for long journeys, meant to be eaten slowly, steadily, as the scenery drifts by in softened, muted tones.

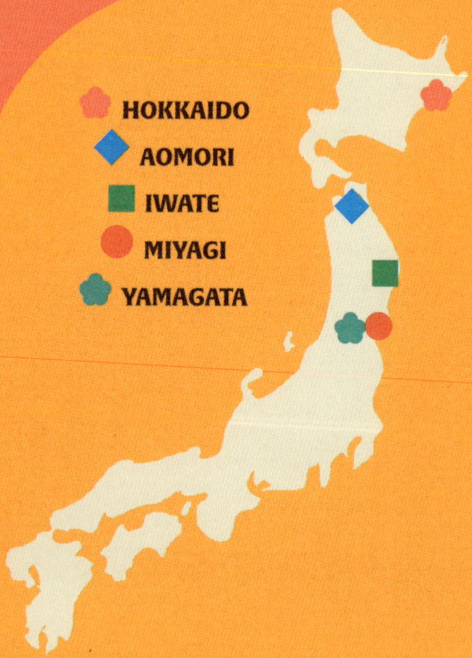

ほたて めし

金格ハンバーグと牛あぶり焼き弁当

むすび丸

牛たん
弁当

牛肉どまん中
BEEF DOMANNAKA

HOKKAIDO

Japan's northernmost island is a land of extremes, where sea meets snow and the seasons shape both life and cuisine. Winters are long and severe, with icy winds blowing from the Sea of Japan and snowdrifts that can bury railways and roads. These conditions define Hokkaido's food culture. Preservation is essential: fish is salted, dried or cured; vegetables are stored in cool cellars. In summer, the landscape shifts – mountains and meadows bloom, rivers swell, and Wagyu cattle graze once more on open pastures.

Hokkaido's capital, Sapporo, is a city shaped equally by survival and celebration. Survival takes the form of Chikaho, a 520 metre (1700 feet) underground walkway that shelters residents from winter's worst weather conditions. Celebration arrives daily from the sea: crabs, scallops, oysters and sea urchin are hauled from cold northern waters, often at prices far easier to swallow than in Tokyo.

At Nijo Market, the air carries the scent of salt, brine and bowls of kaisen-don, a rice bowl filled to the brim with glistening raw seafood – a fleeting taste of this harsh yet bountiful environment. The island's dairy is equally renowned: milk, cream and cheese carry the sweetness of alpine pastures and the endurance of livestock raised through long, snowy winters.

HOKKAIDO PREFECTURE

Akkeshi Station, Hokkaido · 厚岸駅、北海道

43.0562° N, 144.8412° E

UJIIE KAKI MESHI

Ujiie oyster rice · 氏家かきめし

Hokkaido's cold, pristine waters produce some of Japan's sweetest and largest seafood – scallops, sea urchin and seaweed that taste unmistakably of the open sea. Its oysters are among the most prized in the country: plump and tender, with a mild, creamy flavour that makes them especially well suited to cooking.

First created in 1917 at Akkeshi Station in eastern Hokkaido, Ujiie Kaki Meshi showcases those oysters at their best. They are gently simmered at a low temperature to preserve their shape and moisture. Local fishermen once cooked oysters this way for lunch, and the dish was adopted into ekiben form. More than a century later, the same recipe still captures the essence of the northern coast. Simple luxury.

Opening the lid

1. ASARI (PAGE 41)

A handful of Hokkaido clams, braised in their cooking liquid with sake and strongly flavoured with ginger and soy. They bring a pleasantly chewy texture to the ekiben.

2. KAKI (PAGE 40)

Large Hokkaido oysters, gently simmered until tender. Even those wary of fresh oysters may be surprised by them here. Their oceanic flavour sits comfortably alongside the other bento ingredients.

3. FUKI

Fuki – or Japanese butterbur – is a type of sansai (mountain vegetable). It has thick, crunchy stems with a light bitterness. In Ujiie Kaki Meshi the fuki has been braised in dashi to soften and mellow its flavour.

4. SHIITAKE (PAGE 41)

Braised with the clams, these mushrooms take on a deep soy flavour that holds its own against the oysters and shellfish.

5. TAKIKOMI GOHAN (PAGE 40)

Rice cooked in the oyster braising liquid, lightly savoury with subtle marine depth.

6. TAKUAN

Pickled daikon radish.

7. FUKUJINZUKE

Soy-flavoured pickled vegetables, traditionally tinted with red shiso leaves.

RECIPES ➡

KAKI MESHI

Serves 2

OYSTER RICE・牡蠣飯

Slow-cooked oysters are uncommon in Western cuisine but are widely enjoyed in Japan. Japanese oysters are grown to a large size, allowing them to withstand longer cooking without shrinking, while still remaining juicy and tender. As they simmer, the oysters release their flavour into the cooking liquid, which in turn infuses the rice (called takikomi gohan). For this recipe, use large fresh oysters, or large frozen Japanese oysters that have been thawed.

- 200 g (7 oz) short-grain white rice
- 1 celery stalk (see Note)
- 2 tablespoons salt
- 220 g (8 oz) oysters, shucked
- 200 ml (7 fl oz) dashi (page 23)
- 2 tablespoons soy sauce
- 2 tablespoons mirin
- 1 tablespoon sake
- 1 tablespoon caster (superfine) sugar
- 1 cm (½ in) piece ginger, peeled and grated
- 2 tablespoons hijiki, shio kombu or kizami nori
- 1 teaspoon neutral oil (if using hijiki)

Wash the rice until the water runs clear. Set aside to drain.

Peel the celery and cut into batons 5 mm (¼ in) thick. Rub with half the salt to help the dashi penetrate.

Sprinkle the oysters with the remaining salt, massage gently, then rinse clean. (This step cleans the outside of the oyster and removes any excess slime and odour.)

Prepare a large bowl of iced water. In a small saucepan, bring the dashi, soy sauce, mirin, sake, sugar and ginger to a simmer.

Add the oysters and return to a simmer, then reduce the heat, cover and cook for 5 minutes.

Add the celery and cook for 1 minute, or until just tender but still crisp. Place the saucepan in the bowl of iced water, to stop the oysters and celery overcooking.

Once cooled, drain the oysters and celery, reserving the liquid.

If using the hijiki, heat the oil in a separate small pan and quickly stir-fry the seaweed for about 2 minutes over medium heat. (If using shio kombu or kizami nori, this step is unnecessary.)

Add the washed rice to a donabe, lidded saucepan or rice cooker, along with the hijiki, kombu or nori. Follow the instructions on page 22 to soak and cook the rice. You will need approx. 250–375 ml (1–1½ cups) reserved oyster cooking liquid (or enough liquid to reach the level recommended by the rice cooker manufacturer). You can top up with water or dashi if needed.

Five minutes before the rice finishes cooking, add the oysters and celery to warm through.

Once done, either fold all the ingredients together, or arrange the rice in a bento box, layering the oysters and celery on top. It will keep in the fridge for up to 3 days.

NOTE //

The ekiben traditionally includes Japanese butterbur, known as fuki; here, celery is used instead, offering a similar crunch and freshness. Other green stems, such as choy sum (Chinese flowering cabbage), also work.

ASARI TO SHIITAKE TSUKUDANI

Serves 4 as a small side

CLAM AND SHIITAKE TSUKUDANI • あさりと椎茸の佃煮

Slowly braising seafood and vegetables in soy and mirin is a common form of preservation in Japanese kitchens and is a technique that is often used in bento. The seasoning is deliberately strong – heavy on soy and sugar – helping the mixture keep longer, while also serving as a concentrated condiment for rice. Because of this, you will only need to use a small amount.

- 6 dried shiitake mushrooms
- 500 g (1 lb 2 oz) littleneck clams, purged of sand (or about 150 g/5½ oz clam meat)
- 125 ml (½ cup) sake
- 1 tablespoon neutral oil
- 1 thumb-sized piece ginger, peeled and julienned
- 2 tablespoons caster (superfine) sugar
- 90 ml (3 fl oz) soy sauce
- 60 ml (¼ cup) mirin

Place the dried shiitake in a heatproof bowl, cover with hot water and leave the mushrooms to rehydrate for 15 minutes.

Heat a saucepan over high heat. When a drop of water sizzles instantly, add the clams and sake. Cover, reduce the heat and steam for 3–5 minutes, until the clams open.

Set a colander over a bowl and pour in the clams and liquid.

When cool enough to handle, remove the clam meat and discard the shells. Strain the cooking liquid through a very fine mesh sieve or muslin cloth to remove any sand. Reserve 125 ml (½ cup) of the liquid for braising.

Drain the shiitake mushrooms, reserving 60 ml (¼ cup) of the soaking liquid.

Heat the oil in a clean saucepan over medium heat. Add the ginger and stir-fry for 1 minute, then add the clams and mushrooms and cook, uncovered, for a further minute.

Add the reserved clam liquid, mushroom liquid, sugar, soy sauce and mirin. Bring to the boil, skim off any scum, then simmer, uncovered, for 20 minutes, until the liquid reduces slightly and the clams are deeply flavoured.

Remove from the heat and allow to cool. Slice the shiitake finely and place in a container with the clams. Pour the brining liquid over, ensuring everything is submerged. Press down with a small piece of plastic wrap if needed.

Store, covered, in the fridge for up to 10 days.

ワンマン津軽五所川原
ワンマン
走れ
メロス
105
津軽

AOMORI

Known for its rugged coastline, Aomori sits at the northern tip of Honshu. In summer, the city hosts the Nebuta Festival, when towering illuminated floats parade through the streets, accompanied by traditional music, song and dance.

It is difficult to visit Aomori without encountering apples in some form. From cider to pies and jams, apples appear throughout the region's omiyage (souvenirs). The city's mascot, Ikube, is a blue fairy wearing an apple blossom hat – a playful nod to Aomori's name (which translates literally to 'blue-green forest') and its most famous crop.

Aomori and neighbouring Akita also produce some of Japan's best rice and it's a common gift from those travelling in the area. Local rice is an excellent accompaniment to the sweet shellfish and abundant mountain vegetables that come from this part of Japan.

AOMORI PREFECTURE

Shin-Aomori Station, Aomori・新青森駅、青森県

40.8282° N, 140.6935° E

HOTATE MESHI

Scallop rice・ほたてめし

This simple ekiben from Aomori showcases the region's prized scallops, paired with mountain vegetables and kinshi tamago (page 27). It carries the Michinoku stamp, indicating the use of local ingredients and cooking methods from the Tohoku region (Michinoku was the ancient name for the Tohoku area). There is also a Michinoku Coastal Trail running between Hachinohe in Aomori Prefecture and Soma in Fukushima. Unlike most Japanese hiking routes, which tend to run inland, this trail follows a dramatic coastline. It was opened in 2019 to encourage tourism in areas affected by the Tohoku earthquake.

Opening the lid

1. SANSAI

Aomori is shaped not only by the sea, but also by the rugged forests of northern Honshu, where wild mountain vegetables, known collectively as sansai, are foraged. Many varieties appear in local markets, often accompanied by notes on flavour and the best techniques for preparation. They are commonly simmered in dashi, or lightly fried as tempura.

2. HOTATE (PAGE 46)

Large Aomori scallops are gently simmered in dashi until just cooked, retaining their tenderness. In this ekiben the scallops are left whole, with their skirt still attached, adding a pleasantly chewy texture and depth of flavour.

3. KINSHI TAMAGO (PAGE 27)

Finely shredded omelette that has been lightly sweetened tops the layer of rice.

4. TAKIKOMI GOHAN (PAGE 46)

Local Aomori rice is cooked in the scallop broth, which gives it a sweetness and savoury depth.

RECIPES ➡

HOTATE MESHI

Serves 2

SCALLOP RICE・ほたて飯

At its core, this is a basic takikomi gohan – rice cooked with seasoned broth and ingredients. The method is adaptable: any protein that benefits from gentle cooking and releases flavour into the liquid will work. Chicken thighs, mussels, oysters or oily fish such as salmon or trout are all suitable. Vegetables that hold their shape over longer cooking, including carrots, bamboo shoots, burdock root and mushrooms, can be cut into bite-sized pieces and added as well.

5 g (⅛ oz) hijiki (or use an additional 5 g/⅛ oz shio kombu)

200 g (7 oz) short-grain white rice

200 ml (7 fl oz) dashi (page 23)

100 g (3½ oz) baby scallops, with roe and skirt if possible (see Note)

2 tablespoons soy sauce

5 g (⅛ oz) shio kombu

¼ cup mixed diced vegetables (such as carrots, bamboo shoots, burdock root and mushrooms)

Soak the hijiki in warm water for 5 minutes, then drain and set aside. (If using only shio kombu, there is no need to soak it.)

Wash the rice until the water runs clear. Set aside to drain.

Bring the dashi to a simmer in a small saucepan. Add the scallops and soy sauce and reduce the heat. Poach gently for 5 minutes, then turn the heat off and allow to cool.

Add the washed rice to a donabe, lidded saucepan or rice cooker along with the hijiki, shio kombu, vegetables and scallops. Follow the instructions on page 22 to soak and cook the rice. You will need approx. 250–375 ml (1–1½ cups) reserved scallop poaching liquid (or enough liquid to reach the level recommended by the rice cooker manufacturer). You can top up with water or dashi if needed.

The aroma of scallops and seaweed is at its best when the lid is first lifted. Lightly fold the rice to fluff up the grains.

Serve immediately, or chill and consume within 3 days.

NOTE //

This recipe relies on high-quality whole scallops. These are often available frozen, with the skirt attached, at Asian grocers. Defrost the scallops in the fridge for 3–6 hours before use. If you can't source baby scallops with the roe and skirt, fresh scallops with roe make a good substitute, as they will add suitable richness and depth.

IWATE

Far from the cultural centres of Kyoto and Tokyo, Iwate developed at its own pace, shaped by farming villages, fishing communities and mountain settlements. This relative isolation fostered a food culture grounded in local produce - grains, roots, preserved vegetables and river fish, ingredients chosen for their ability to endure harsh winters and uncertain harvests.

Morioka, the prefectural capital, sits inland at the confluence of the Kitakami, Nakatsu and Shizukuishi rivers. Founded over 400 years ago to control key trade routes, the city remains distant from the sea, and fresh seafood plays a smaller role in daily cooking. Instead, grilled chicken restaurants are common, alongside noodle specialists serving local favourites: jajamen, thick noodles in a meat and dark bean sauce inspired by Chinese zhajiangmian; reimen, chilled noodles in beef broth influenced by Korean naengmyeon; and wanko soba, served in tiny, continuous portions as a playful test of endurance.

Morioka is also known for its unhurried pace. Kissaten dot the city, offering quiet refuge from winter cold or summer heat. These old-style coffee houses offer hand-drip coffee and thick slices of buttered shokupan toast. Few pleasures rival lingering in a Morioka cafe - sipping a meticulously prepared coffee while watching Somei Yoshino cherry trees sway along the Nakatsu River.

IWATE PREFECTURE

Ichinoseki Station, Iwate・一ノ関駅、岩手県

38.9262° N, 141.1376° E

KINKAKU HANBAGU TO GYU ABURI YAKI BENTO

Gold-standard hamburg and grilled beef bento・金格ハンバーグと牛あぶり焼き弁当

This meat-forward bento features grilled beef, gently stewed beef tendons that have been simmered in a sweet and spicy sauce with soy and Japanese pepper, and is topped with Kakunoshin's original Kinkaku hamburg steak.

Kakunoshin is a specialist butcher and restaurant known for Iwate prefecture's brand, Kanzaki Aged Meat. From their base in Ichinoseki, they serve aged beef at restaurants in both Ichinoseki and Tokyo, as well as through their online shop.

Unlike many hamburg steaks sold commercially, this one is served without sauce – such is the maker's confidence that the meat is juicy and flavourful enough to stand on its own. The Kinkaku Hamburg is made exclusively with Iwate ingredients, including local beef and the prefecture's branded Hakkinton Pork. The meat is marinated in house-made salt koji to deepen its flavour and tenderness. Thoroughly researched and carefully refined, this hamburg has won numerous food awards and has become a signature of the shop.

Opening the lid

1. HAMBURG (PAGE 52)
A blend of pork and beef mince with a gentle onion sweetness. Unlike American hamburgers, these are mixed with spices and breadcrumbs resulting in a patty that's soft, juicy and deeply savoury. It is the undisputed centrepiece of this bento.

2. GYUNIKU ABURI YAKI
Beef seared quickly over high heat to release aroma and flavour without fully cooking through, keeping it tender and supple.

3. GYUSUJI NIKOMI (PAGE 53)
Lightly braised beef tendon with a mild, rounded flavour. No single element dominates, allowing the bento to remain balanced and cohesive.

4. KINOKO-NI
Shimeji and king oyster (eryngii) mushrooms, gently braised, offering an earthy sweetness that complements the beef.

5. KOMBU-NI
Shredded kombu adds umami and texture, a practical and flavourful way to reuse kombu after making dashi.

6. NOZAWANA
Leafy greens, similar to turnip tops, simply stir-fried to provide freshness and contrast.

7. BENISHOGA
Pickled ginger for brightness, crunch and a sharp counterpoint to the richness of the meat.

RECIPES ➡

HAMBURG

ハンバーグ

Makes 2 large or 4 small patties

Hamburg steak is a dish deeply embedded in Japanese home cooking, taught in schools and endlessly adapted in households across the country. Its suitability for bento lies in the addition of milk and panko breadcrumbs, which keep the meat patties light and moist, even when eaten cold. The panko absorbs both fat and seasoning, ensuring each bite remains flavourful.

Although unadorned in this ekiben, hamburg is often served with homemade tomato sauce, demi-glace or simply ketchup.

15 g (½ oz) butter
½ onion, finely diced
25 ml (¾ fl oz) milk
1 egg
30 g (½ cup) panko breadcrumbs
125 g (4½ oz) minced (ground) beef (see Note)
125 g (4½ oz) minced (ground) pork
1 tablespoon tomato ketchup
½ teaspoon ground nutmeg
½ teaspoon salt
½ teaspoon ground black pepper
2 tablespoons neutral oil

Melt the butter in a frying pan over medium–low heat. Add the onion and cook gently for about 10 minutes, until softened but not browned. Remove from the pan and allow to cool.

While the onion is cooking, combine the milk, egg and panko in a bowl.

Once the onion has cooled, add it to the panko mixture, along with the minced meat, ketchup, nutmeg, salt and pepper. Mix until the meat becomes sticky. Shape into two large or four small ovals, lightly slapping each between your hands to expel air, then press a shallow indent into the centre to encourage even cooking.

Heat a lidded frying pan over medium heat and add the oil. Place the hamburg steaks in the pan, then cover and cook for 3 minutes. Turn, cover again, and cook for a further 3 minutes, or until well coloured on both sides. Remove to a plate.

Insert a skewer into the centre to check doneness; the skewer should feel hot to the touch. If necessary, return the hamburg steaks to the pan and cook for another 1–2 minutes.

Once cooked through, transfer to a plate and serve immediately, or allow to cool and refrigerate. Consume within 2 days.

NOTE //

You can use only beef or pork mince if you prefer.

GYUSUJI NIKOMI

Serves 4

BRAISED BEEF TENDON・牛すじ煮込み

The 'tendon' used here is not pure connective tissue, but sinewy cuts that benefit from long, gentle cooking. Cuts often sold as 'gravy beef' – shin, shoulder, neck or brisket – work well, provided they contain enough sinew to develop a gelatinous, silky texture. Some or all of the tendon can be replaced with sliced beef if desired.

- 500 g (1 lb 2 oz) beef tendon or sinewy beef, cut in half or into large chunks
- 1 spring onion (scallion), green part only
- 1 thumb-sized piece ginger, sliced
- 1 tablespoon sake
- sansho pepper, to serve

FINISHING SAUCE

- 100 ml (3½ fl oz) sake
- 70 ml (2¼ fl oz) soy sauce
- 30 ml (1 fl oz) mirin
- 1 tablespoon zarame or caster (superfine) sugar

Place the beef in a saucepan and cover with water. Bring to the boil and cook for 5 minutes, then drain and rinse thoroughly.

Transfer the beef to a clean saucepan and cover with fresh water. Add the spring onion, ginger and sake. Bring to the boil, then reduce the heat and simmer for 1 hour, or until the beef is tender.

Drain the beef, reserving 400 ml (14 fl oz) of the cooking liquid. Discard the aromatics and allow the beef to cool.

When cool enough to handle, cut into bite-sized pieces.

Return the beef to a clean saucepan, along with the reserved cooking liquid and the finishing sauce ingredients. Braise gently for a further 30 minutes, skimming regularly.

Serve immediately, or allow to cool, then refrigerate for up to 4 days. If chilled, the fat will solidify on the surface and can be removed for a cleaner finish.

Sprinkle with sansho before serving.

IWATE PREFECTURE

Ichinoseki Station, Iwate・一ノ関駅、岩手県

38.9262° N, 141.1376° E

KEIMAI BENTO

Bird dance bento・鶏舞弁当

From Iwate, a region long associated with high-quality poultry, comes Keimai Bento. The name is taken from keimai, a performing art that is common in the city of Ichinoseki ('kei' is also the local word for 'chicken'). With vigorous jumps, stamping steps and driving drums, the dance is performed at shrine festivals as a ritual prayer for good harvests, health and protection. Rooted in farming culture, it reflects the deep local reverence for poultry as both sustenance and a symbol of vitality. One of the dancers is illustrated on the bento label, a reprint of a woodblock print carved by Fujio Sato, wearing the tall, ornate headpieces that evoke the crest and movement of a rooster.

As befitting the label, this bento highlights the quality of the local poultry by keeping the preparation simple. The chicken is grilled and lightly coated with a thin teriyaki glaze, just enough to retain moisture and enhance flavour without masking the quality of the meat.

The bento also includes miso shiso maki, a regional specialty made from Sendai miso, sugar and walnuts, wrapped in green shiso leaves and fried. Sendai miso was once so valuable that the warlord Date Masamune (1567–1636) is said to have built a miso storehouse within the walls of his castle. Today, miso shiso maki is a familiar side dish and bar snack across the region, its salty richness well suited to accompanying alcohol.

The bento ingredients are all served atop locally grown Hitomebore rice.

Opening the lid

1. TORI TERIYAKI (PAGE 56)

Perhaps surprisingly, the grilled chicken in this bento is very lightly sauced. This restraint allows the flavour of the chicken itself to remain front and centre.

2. KINSHI TAMAGO (PAGE 27)

The classic pairing of chicken and egg in this ekiben recalls dishes such as oyakodon (chicken and egg rice bowl, a classic Japanese comfort food). Here, finely sliced omelette which has been sweetened with mirin and sugar, echoes the sweet flavours of the teriyaki chicken.

3. MISO SHISO MAKI (PAGE 57)

Miso cooked with sugar and walnuts, wrapped in shiso leaf and fried, creates a herbaceous balance of saltiness and sweetness.

4. NIMONO (PAGE 29)

Shiitake mushrooms and bamboo shoots simmered in dashi contribute depth of umami and textural contrast.

5. SASA KAMABOKO

A local fish cake once made from flounder, and now more commonly from pollock. Traditionally hand-shaped to resemble a bamboo leaf (sasa), it is today moulded, skewered and lightly grilled for a browned surface. It may be served as a side, as here, or as an appetiser with soy sauce, wasabi or plum paste.

6. TSUKEMONO

Vegetable pickles such as miso zuke daikon (daikon pickled in miso) and sakura-zuke (pink pickled radish) provide acidity and freshness.

RECIPES ➡

TORI TERIYAKI

Serves 2

TERIYAKI CHICKEN・照り焼きチキン

A favourite worldwide yet surprisingly uncommon in Japan, teriyaki chicken is typically grilled and finished with a glossy, sweetened soy glaze. While the chicken is sometimes marinated beforehand, this version is seasoned simply with salt and glazed at the end, allowing the flavour of the local poultry to remain clear.

- 2 boneless chicken thighs, skin on
- 1 teaspoon salt
- 2 tablespoons neutral oil
- 1 tablespoon soy sauce
- 1 tablespoon mirin
- 1 tablespoon sake
- 1 tablespoon water
- 1 teaspoon caster (superfine) sugar
- ½ teaspoon potato starch

Pierce the chicken thighs with a fork and season evenly with the salt.

Heat a lidded frying pan over medium-high heat and add the oil. Add the chicken, skin side down, and cook for about 5 minutes, until well coloured.

Meanwhile, mix the remaining ingredients in a small bowl.

Turn the chicken over and pour the sauce into the pan, taking care as it may splatter. Reduce the heat to low, then cover and cook for a further 5 minutes, or until cooked through and lightly glazed.

The chicken will keep covered in the fridge for 2 days.

MISO SHISO MAKI

SWEET SHISO-WRAPPED MISO WITH WALNUTS・味噌しそ巻き

Makes 12 (1–2 pieces per bento)

Perhaps the most unexpectedly delicious element of this bento, miso shiso maki is little more than a shiso leaf, walnuts and miso paste – yet the result is striking. The salty richness of the miso, the subtle sweetness of walnuts and the vegetal freshness of the shiso leaf combine to create an eye-opening intensity of flavour. Miso shiso maki is highly recommended as an accompaniment to simply grilled meat, seafood or vegetables.

- 50 g (½ cup) walnuts
- 50 g (1¾ oz) shiro miso (white miso paste)
- 2 tablespoons caster (superfine) sugar
- 1 tablespoon ground white sesame seeds
- 1 tablespoon plain (all-purpose) flour
- pinch of shichimi togarashi
- 1 tablespoon neutral oil, plus extra for pan-frying
- 12 green shiso (oba) leaves

Finely chop the walnuts by hand or using a food processor.

Place the chopped walnuts in a small saucepan. Add the miso paste, sugar, sesame seeds, flour, shichimi and oil. Mix well, then cook over medium heat for 3–4 minutes, until aromatic. Add a little water or reduce the heat if the mixture becomes too dry, you are aiming for a thick paste consistency, like peanut butter.

Remove from the heat and allow to cool, then divide into 12 portions. At this point you can either store the miso mixture in the fridge (see below), or roll the miso into the shiso leaves.

Shape into small cylinders and place one on each shiso leaf. Roll up and secure each portion with a toothpick.

Heat a large frying pan over medium heat and add enough oil to coat the surface. Fry the rolls, turning regularly, for 2–3 minutes, until the leaves are browned.

Drain on paper towel, remove the toothpicks and serve.

The miso mixture will last for up to 1 week in an airtight container in the fridge (see Note).

Rolled and fried miso shiso maki should be consumed within 1 day.

NOTE //

You can use any leftover miso as a dip for vegetables.

MIYAGI

Sendai, the capital of Miyagi and the largest city in the country's scenic northeast region of Tohoku, is known as the 'City of Trees'. Miyagi is a prefecture where wide avenues lined with zelkova (Japanese elm trees) meet the cool air that drifts in from Matsushima Bay. Founded by the samurai lord Date Masamune, the city of Sendai lies just 90 minutes by Shinkansen from Tokyo, yet retains a distinct food culture shaped by resilience, seasonal clarity and respect for ingredients.

The surrounding waters yield some of Japan's finest seafood. Oysters from nearby bays are plump and briny, while sardines and mackerel appear at their peak in local cooking. Inland, Miyagi's rice is prized for its balance in flavour and gentle sweetness, forming the backbone of everyday meals and bento alike.

Sendai is best known for gyutan – thick-cut beef tongue that has been grilled over charcoal, seasoned simply with salt, and served with barley rice and oxtail soup. Originally a postwar invention, gyutan has become a symbol of the city, its smoky aroma drifting from specialty restaurants clustered around the station. Across the prefecture, light soy, mild sweetness and restrained seasoning allow ingredients to speak for themselves.

MIYAGI PREFECTURE

Sendai Station, Miyagi・仙台駅、宮城県

38.2604° N, 140.8824° E

MUSUBI MARU BENTO

Musubi Maru bento・むすび丸弁当

With its many small dishes, this ekiben is ideal for travellers keen to sample a wide range of regional foods that are specific to Miyagi. The bento is reflective of the prefecture's geography – a region that has been shaped equally by sea and mountains – as is evident from the variety of seafood, vegetables, rice and preserved specialties that are found within this bento.

Named after the region's official mascot, Musubi Maru, who is depicted with a musubi (rice ball) for a head and dressed in samurai armour – a playful, lighthearted reference to Date Masamune, the famed warlord who founded Sendai – this bento offers a broad introduction to Miyagi's local flavours.

Opening the lid

1. MUSUBI

This rice ball is the visual centrepiece of this bento, made from soft local rice that has been decorated with a nori mouth, black bean eyes, and a strip of yuzu peel forming a crescent helmet.

2. SANMA NO KANRONI (PAGE 62)

Pacific saury braised in a sweet soy sauce. The fish is cooked with bones and innards intact, as the innards are considered a delicacy. The meat becomes tender and easily separates from the bone, with a balanced sweet-savoury flavour.

3. SASA KAMABOKO

A local fish cake shaped like a bamboo leaf (sasa), lightly grilled.

4. RENKON KINPIRA

Lotus root stir-fried in sesame oil, crisp and lightly seasoned to highlight its natural sweetness.

5. SENDAI NAGA NASU ZUKE

Long local eggplants (aubergine) pickled in miso. Their thin skins remain tender after pickling, and specialty shops sell them as edible regional souvenirs.

6. TORI NIKU NO SAKE KASU (SENDAI) MISO ZUKE YAKI (PAGE 63)

Chicken thighs marinated in sake kasu (sake lees) and Sendai miso, then grilled. The marinade tenderises the meat and caramelises on the surface, giving a gentle sweetness and depth.

7. HARAKO MESHI (PAGE 64)

A celebrated local dish of salmon rice topped with salmon roe. 'Hara' is the regional word for salmon, while 'harako' refers to its eggs. The dish is said to have been served to Date Masamune during inspections of the Arahama Canal.

Salmon is simmered simply in soy-seasoned water, which is then used to cook the rice. The cooked rice is then topped with the salmon and marinated roe.

8. ANZU NO SHIROPPU-ZUKE

Apricot gently cooked in syrup, offering a sweet-tart finish that refreshes the palate.

9. SENDAI MISO AME

A local miso candy, balancing sweet and salty flavours to close the meal.

RECIPES ➡

SANMA NO KANRONI

Serves 4

PACIFIC SAURY BRAISED IN A SWEET SAUCE・秋刀魚の甘露煮

Pacific saury (sanma) is at its best in autumn, when it's fattiest and most flavourful. It is a rich, oily fish, similar to mackerel and sardines, though it is slightly milder in flavour. Outside Japan it can be difficult to source, though some Asian grocers carry frozen sanma. Mackerel is a suitable substitute, with enough oiliness to remain tender through the cooking process, and enough flavour to stand up to the marinade.

4 small sanma, about 80 g (2¾ oz) each, or 2 large sanma, about 150 g (5½ oz) each
1 tablespoon rice vinegar
100 ml (3½ fl oz) water
3 tablespoons sake
3 tablespoons mirin
2 tablespoons soy sauce
1 tablespoon caster (superfine) sugar
1 dried chilli, seeds removed
1 thumb-sized piece ginger, finely sliced into 2–3 mm (⅛ in) rounds

Rub the skin of the fish to remove any scales and slime, then cut off the head and tail. (If using mackerel, also remove the innards.)

Cut each fish through the bone into three pieces if small, or four if large.

Place the fish in cold water with the rice vinegar, massage gently, then rinse. (This step helps remove some of the 'fishiness'.)

In a saucepan, combine the water, sake, mirin, soy sauce, sugar and chilli. Bring to the boil, then add the fish in one layer, top with the ginger, adding more water if necessary to submerge the fish. Return to the boil, then reduce the heat and cover with a cartouche (a round of baking paper with a small hole cut in the centre).

Simmer gently for 30 minutes. Serve immediately, or cool in the liquid and refrigerate for up to 3 days.

TORI NIKU NO SAKE KASU (SENDAI) MISO ZUKE YAKI

Serves 2 as a main or 4 as part of a shared meal

GRILLED CHICKEN MARINATED IN SAKE KASU AND SENDAI MISO・鶏肉の酒粕(仙台)味噌漬け焼き

This pleasantly sweet and salty meat preparation brings together miso and sake, two of Tohoku's prized products. The complexity from the sake kasu imparts a subtle fruity aroma to the chicken. The chicken can be substituted for pork or fish if desired.

You will need to begin this recipe the day before to allow the chicken to marinate.

- 2 tablespoons shiro miso (white miso paste)
- 2 tablespoons sake kasu (sake lees)
- 2 tablespoons caster (superfine) sugar
- 1 tablespoon shio koji
- 1 tablespoon sake
- 1 tablespoon mirin
- 2 boneless chicken thighs, skin on or off
- 2 tablespoons neutral oil

Mix together the miso, sake kasu, sugar, shio koji, sake and mirin.

Spread half the mixture in a container. Lay a piece of muslin over the paste, place the chicken on top, cover with another cloth, and spread the remaining marinade over.

Cover and refrigerate overnight.

Remove the chicken from the marinade, discarding the marinade. Heat the oil in a frying pan over medium heat and cook the chicken, skin side down, for 5 minutes. Turn and cook for a further 5 minutes, or until cooked through.

Rest briefly, then cut into bite-sized pieces. The chicken will keep in the fridge for 2 days.

HARAKO MESHI

Serves 4

SALMON ROE RICE・はらこ飯

This is a centuries-old dish from when Date Masamune inspected the construction of the Arahama Canal, a major project providing transportation as well as water to farmland. It was originally a special dish made using autumn-harvested wild salmon, but now, with salmon so common, you can make it anytime.

- 400 g (14 oz) salmon fillet, skin removed
- 200 ml (7 fl oz) water
- 3 slices ginger
- 2 tablespoons soy sauce
- 2 tablespoons mirin
- 300 g (10½ oz) short-grain white rice
- 5 cm (2 in) piece kombu
- kinshi tamago (page 27), to serve
- 2 tablespoons ikura (see below)

IKURA

- 50 g (1¾ oz) salmon roe
- 2 tablespoons sake
- 1 tablespoon mirin
- 1 tablespoon soy sauce

To prepare the ikura, gently rinse the salmon roe under cold water to remove the surface membrane and drain.

Rinse the salmon roe briefly in 1 tablespoon of the sake, then drain once more.

Mix the roe with the mirin, soy sauce and remaining 1 tablespoon of the sake. Cover and refrigerate for 3 hours. Drain off the marinade and refrigerate in a covered container; the ikura will keep for up to 5 days.

Meanwhile, wash the rice until the water runs clear. Set aside to drain.

Cut the salmon into four even pieces. Bring the water, ginger, soy sauce and mirin to a simmer in a frying pan. Add the salmon and cook for 5 minutes, or until just done.

Remove from the heat and allow to cool. Gently lift out the salmon and set aside.

Add the washed rice to a donabe, lidded saucepan or rice cooker along with the kombu. Follow the instructions on page 22 to soak and cook the rice. You will need approx. 375–400 ml (1½ cups–13½ fl oz) reserved salmon cooking liquid (or enough liquid to reach the level recommended by the rice cooker manufacturer).

Five minutes before the rice finishes cooking, add the salmon to warm through.

Serve topped with kinshi tamago and the ikura. Once assembled, the bento will keep in the fridge for up to 2 days.

MIYAGI PREFECTURE

Sendai Station, Miyagi · 仙台駅、宮城県

38.2604° N, 140.8824° E

SUMIBI YAKI FU GYUTAN BENTO

Charcoal grilled-style beef tongue bento · 炭火焼風牛たん弁当

This is a special ekiben, the only one in this book to include an internal heating device. Once the pull tab is activated, the bento warms itself within minutes, delivering a meal that feels like it has been freshly cooked – a practical luxury well suited to grilled meat as the fat melts and makes it more tender.

The city of Sendai is the birthplace of this style of grilled beef tongue. The dish was created here in 1948, in the years following World War II. At the time, chickens were scarce and competition among restaurants was fierce. At Aji Tasuke, a yakitori restaurant in the city, chef Keishiro Sano searched for an alternative ingredient that could define his shop. After extensive experimentation, he perfected the method of cutting and grilling beef tongue, sourcing local beef wherever possible. Aji Tasuke still operates today and remains extremely popular – expect a queue if you wish to taste the original Sendai gyutan.

In Sendai, gyutan is typically served at restaurants with barley rice, oxtail soup that has been heavily seasoned with spring onions (scallions), braised beef tendon, grated yam for mixing into rice, and a refreshing cabbage salad.

The appearance of this gyutan ekiben is strikingly simple: slices of grilled beef tongue laid over rice, accompanied by the signature miso-pickled chilli. Gyutan can be sliced thinly, as in this bento, or cut thick and scored for juiciness and texture. The ekiben uses a cut of tongue called shirotan, a softer, more tender section of the tongue.

Born of necessity, gyutan has become one of Japan's most recognisable regional dishes.

Opening the lid

1. GYUTAN (PAGE 69)

Charcoal-grilled beef tongue, tender yet resilient, with enough structure to lift cleanly with rice. This ekiben comes with a small packet of fine salt to sprinkle over the gyutan for seasoning. Shiogama, a city just north of Sendai, was one of Japan's most famous salt producing areas, producing salt since the Jomon period (at least 1000 BCE). The name of the city literally translates to 'salt furnace', referring to the traditional process of boiling sea water to make salt.

2. MUGI GOHAN (PAGE 70)

Rice steamed with barley, adding nuttiness and texture. Once a frugal addition during difficult times, barley rice is now inseparable from gyutan.

3. NANBANMISOZUKE (PAGE 70)

A boldly spiced miso chilli condiment, salty and pungent, yet fresh from just-cooked chillies that retain their bite.

RECIPES ➡

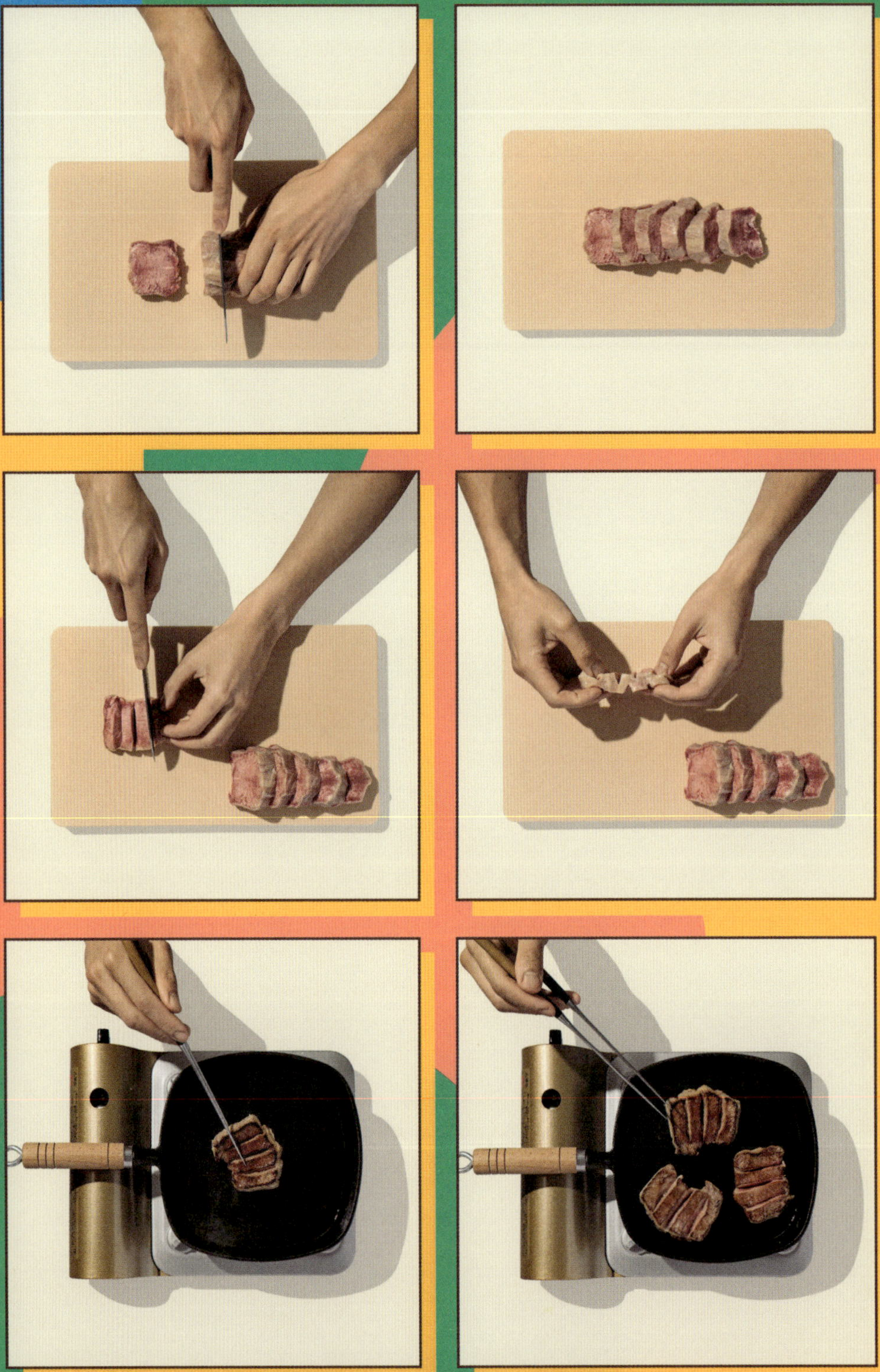

GYUTAN

Serves 8

GRILLED BEEF TONGUE・牛タン

Sendai gyutan is prepared in two main styles: thinly sliced, or thickly cut and cross-hatched to improve tenderness. The thicker cut is more expensive and often considered more luxurious, but must be served hot. Thin slices can be enjoyed hot or cold.

The back of the tongue, known as shirotan (white tongue), is fattier and more tender. Towards the tip is akatan (red tongue), which has a stronger flavour but a firmer texture. White tongue is best suited to thick cuts, while red tongue works well sliced thinly.

You will need to begin this recipe 2 days before serving to allow for the tongue to marinate.

1½ tablespoons salt, plus extra to serve
25 ml (¾ fl oz) sake
25 ml (¾ fl oz) mirin
450 ml (15 fl oz) water
1 × 1.5 kg (3 lb 5 oz) whole beef tongue (about 130–150 g/4½–5½ oz per person)
steamed rice (page 22), to serve

Combine the salt, sake, mirin and water in a saucepan and heat until the salt dissolves. Allow to cool completely.

Using a sharp knife, remove the outer skin from the beef tongue. Trim the underside and reserve it for braising.

Place the tongue in a large, airtight zip-lock bag, then pour in the marinade. Remove as much air as possible then seal and refrigerate for 2 days.

After marinating, remove the tongue from the liquid. Discard the liquid and pat the tongue dry with paper towel.

THIN CUT

Slice the tongue very thinly, about 3–4 mm (⅛–¼ in) thick.

Preheat a chargrill or frying pan over medium-high heat and cook the tongue slices for 2–3 minutes on each side, until well coloured.

Serve immediately, with rice and a little extra salt on the side to adjust the seasoning as you wish.

Thin-cut gyutan will keep in the fridge for 1 day.

THICK CUT

Slice the tongue into 1 cm (½ in) pieces. Make four vertical cuts about 70 per cent of the way through the meat. Turn the meat over, then make three more cuts on the reverse side, offset to form a zigzag pattern.

Preheat a chargrill or frying pan over medium heat and cook the tongue for 3–5 minutes on each side, until well coloured.

Remove from the heat and slice across the zigzag cuts to yield thick, tender pieces.

Serve immediately, with rice and a little extra salt.

MUGI GOHAN

Serves 4

BARLEY RICE・麦ご飯

Cooked with a ratio of three parts rice to one part barley, this barley rice is the essential accompaniment to gyutan (page 69). The barley adds a nutty flavour and firm texture that stands up well to the rich beef tongue.

To calculate the amount of water needed, use your usual amount for the rice, then add double the weight of the barley in additional water. For example, if 300 g (10½ oz) rice typically requires 360 ml (12 fl oz) water, add an extra 200 ml (7 fl oz) water for 100 g (3½ oz) of barley, for a total of 560 ml (2¼ cups).

300 g (10½ oz) short-grain white rice
100 g (3½ oz) hulled barley
560 ml (19 fl oz) water

Wash the rice and barley together until the water runs clear. Set aside to drain.

Add the washed rice and barley to a donabe, lidded saucepan or rice cooker along with the water. Follow the instructions on page 22 to soak and cook the rice.

The rice mixture will keep in the fridge for 2 days.

NANBANMISOZUKE

Makes about 250 ml (1 cup)

MISO CHILLI RELISH・南蛮味噌漬け

This is the spiciest recipe in the book: chillies cut into small pieces, quickly stir-fried, then marinated in a sweet miso mixture. The result is hot, fragrant, fresh and lightly sweet, making it an ideal companion to fatty meats.

1 tablespoon neutral oil
12 long red or green chillies, seeds removed, cut into roughly 1 cm (½ in) pieces
30 ml (1 fl oz) sake
30 ml (1 fl oz) mirin
1 tablespoon caster (superfine) sugar
80 g (2¾ oz) shiro miso (white miso paste)
1 teaspoon sesame oil
1 garlic clove, minced

Heat a frying pan or wok over high heat and add the oil. When smoking, stir-fry the chillies for just a minute or two until lightly charred, then transfer to a plate to cool. The chillies should retain some crunch.

In a saucepan, bring the sake and mirin to the boil to evaporate the alcohol. Stir in the sugar, miso, sesame oil and garlic. Remove from the heat and allow the mixture to cool, then combine with the chillies.

Pack tightly into a container and refrigerate for up to 1 week.

INTERVIEW WITH
JR EAST CROSS

'Ekiben are beloved as a product that symbolises the joy and prosperity of travel, and today ... they have become a cultural hub that brings together and serves diverse regional flavours from all over Japan.'

EKIBEN BUSINESS

JR East Cross (also known as JR Cross) operates a number of Japanese and Western restaurants inside train stations, as well as the popular NewDays convenience stores. They are a large ekiben manufacturer, having merged with various smaller ekiben manufacturers.

I had the pleasure of talking to Mai Nakamura, the public relations officer for JR East Cross Station Foods Company, and learning about the company's history, processes and how they see the future of ekiben.

Q: *HOW DID YOUR COMPANY'S EKIBEN BUSINESS BEGIN?*

A:

The origins of the ekiben business are deeply connected to the efforts of our predecessor, Nihon Shokudo Co., Ltd. (established in 1938), to continue providing meals to long-distance passengers amid the severe food shortages caused by the intensification of the Pacific War. Starting in July 1941, as the wartime conditions worsened, the number of dining cars on long-distance trains was reduced. Furthermore, on 1 April, 1944, the attachment of dining cars to trains was discontinued.

In response to this, the Gomoku Bento (mixed bento) was launched on the same day, to ensure meals for long-distance passengers. The sale of this Gomoku Bento marked the beginning of the company's current on-train sales. At the time, rice was rationed, so Gomoku Bento differed from today's gomoku gohan (rice with mixed ingredients), and was a simple mix of meat, fish and vegetables. However, the bento was well received by passengers during a time of food shortages. Thus, the ekiben business began as part of railway services, aiming to continue providing meals to passengers during the extremely difficult circumstances of wartime shortages.

Q: *WHAT WERE THE SALES METHODS AT THE TIME?*

A:

The main sales locations were from train windows at train departure stations (Tokyo, Ueno, Wakkanai, Nagasaki) and at stations with station cafeterias (Otaru, Hakodate, Sendai, Matsumoto, Ryogoku, Shimbashi, Osaka, Okayama, Hiroshima, Shimonoseki, Kumamoto). Initially, sales locations were strictly limited. Purchasers were also required to show a long-distance ticket or travel documents, and priority was given to disabled veterans and the elderly.

Q: *HOW HAVE PASSENGERS' TASTES AND PREFERENCES CHANGED OVER TIME?*

A:

Over time, passengers' tastes and preferences for ekiben and the food served at stations have shifted significantly, from an era of enduring shortages to a desire for abundance, speed, health and variety.

Q: *WHAT ARE SOME INNOVATIONS, INGREDIENTS OR TECHNIQUES THAT MAKE EKIBEN UNIQUE?*

A:

Unlike everyday bento or takeaway bento, ekiben are meant to be eaten cold. The ingredients and cooking methods are carefully selected to ensure they remain delicious even when served cold. For example, when grilling fish or meat, they are cooked using high-temperature steam rather than fire. By wrapping the ingredients in steam and cooking them quickly at a high temperature, the surface is crispy and golden brown, while the interior is soft and fluffy, ensuring a pleasant texture even when cold. Also, since rice tends to dry out when cooled due to the low temperature and humidity in winter, the amount of water and the cooking time are adjusted depending on the season.

Ekiben are also unique in that they come with wrapping paper and sleeves. Because the contents are hidden, the design is carefully crafted to make the contents clear at a glance. They are designed with tight packaging to prevent ingredients from shifting during transportation.

Q: *WHAT FACTORS DO YOU PRIORITISE WHEN DEVELOPING PRODUCTS?*

A:

As well as prioritising the cooking method and flavours for eating dishes cold, we also place importance on developing products that allow you to experience a culinary journey through Japan. Over the years, a wide variety of ekiben have appeared, including those made with seasonal ingredients, local specialties, and those that can be heated. Since Japan has four seasons – spring, summer, fall and winter – we have designed and developed several products to match each season. These are products that allow you to immerse yourself in the season.

Q: *WHAT DO YOU THINK MAKES EKIBEN A SPECIAL PART OF JAPANESE CULTURE AND TRAVEL?*

A:

It lies in their long history as a part of the railway business and their cultural symbolism, reflecting the changing social conditions of Japan. Ekiben are beloved as a product that symbolises the joy and prosperity of travel, and today, as exemplified by Tokyo Station's Ekiben Matsuri (page 74), they have become a cultural hub that brings together and serves diverse regional flavours from all over Japan. Furthermore, with Washoku (traditional

Japanese cuisine) being registered as a UNESCO Intangible Cultural Heritage, ekiben have attracted attention overseas as a uniquely Japanese food culture.

Q: *WHAT ARE THE MAJOR TRENDS IN THE EKIBEN MARKET TODAY?*

A:

With the increasing number of travellers travelling to tourist destinations by Shinkansen and limited express trains, inbound demand in particular is on the rise. Popular ekiben products among inbound tourists include makunouchi bento (beautifully presented and often in Japanese-style packaging), which offer a uniquely Japanese dining experience, eel bento, heated bento (beef tongue and other dishes that can be heated and eaten), Tonkatsu and Edo misokatsu beef suki. In particular, heated bento have seen an increase in the variety of options available and are selling well.

While traditional ekiben tend to be overwhelmingly popular overall, there are some products that have recently attracted attention through social media. The ekiben most affected by social media was the Kamio Bento Club: Engawa Oshizushi, which has become one of the top 10 best-selling items.

We believe that social media has had a major impact on the ekiben market, not only by temporarily increasing sales and unit sales, but also by acquiring new customer segments. There is an increase in young customers in their twenties and the appeal of ekiben is prolonged through the spread of social media posts.

Q: *ARE THERE ANY CHALLENGES YOU CURRENTLY FACE AS AN EKIBEN MANUFACTURER?*

A:

Current challenges include: higher train speeds (and improved train convenience); shorter time spent on trains which reduces demand for in-train meals; eating is possible once you arrive at your destination; decreased number of stops on long-distance trains (limited express and Shinkansen); rising raw material, logistics and labour costs; and labour shortages.

Q: *GIVEN THE DECLINING POPULATION IN RURAL AREAS AND FLUCTUATIONS IN PASSENGER NUMBERS, WHAT ARE YOUR THOUGHTS ON THE FUTURE OF EKIBEN?*

A:

Popular ekiben can now be ordered online, even in areas where they were previously unavailable. Enjoying ekiben at home, anywhere in the country, can give you the feeling of travelling.

Ekiben Matsuri

If you're short on time in Japan and want to get a glimpse of the breadth of ekiben available, head to Ekiben Matsuri in Tokyo Station. Opened in 2012, Ekiben Matsuri brings together approximately 150 ekiben from across the country. The store is open from 5:30 am to 10 pm, which gives you ample time to shop for ekiben.

The store is incredibly popular with locals and tourists, so it's best to get in early for the widest range, but the shelves are restocked regularly and some ekiben appear later in the day, so there's always something to buy. If you see an ekiben you want to try, pick it up, as it might not be there the next time you pass through. The ekiben on offer change regularly so check the website or social media to see what's currently on offer: foods.jr-cross.co.jp/matsuri/.

The freshly made deliciousness is preserved in the freezer, and the cooking method is devised in advance to maintain that deliciousness over time. To maximise flavour, microwave-safe containers are used, with the wooden container designed to absorb excess moisture during heating. The amount of water added is adjusted to prevent the rice from crumbing and technology is used to enhance moisture retention, resulting in a thorough frozen bento design.

Furthermore, by wrapping the plastic bag in the same design as the products sold at train stations, we have realistically recreated the atmosphere of an authentic ekiben, focusing on a taste that evokes the feeling of travel and the tradition and excitement unique to ekiben. We are seeing positive results in expanding ekiben sales channels, primarily through online sales, as gifts for family members living far away.

We are also holding a limited time, off-site special event called the Mobile Ekiben Matsuri (festival), featuring a selection of popular ekiben from the Ekiben Festival.

YAMAGATA

A mountainous prefecture known for some of Japan's finest hiking, Yamagata is shaped by dense forests, heavy snowfall and a deep-rooted food culture. While the region is perhaps best known for its sakuranbo cherries, it is also celebrated for its peaches, wild mountain vegetables and exceptional beef.

The city of Yonezawa, where the Gyuniku Domannaka ekiben originates, lies inland, far from the sea, and its cuisine reflects that geography. Beef and agricultural products such as grapes, cherries, melons and peaches take centre stage here. Visitors are well rewarded exploring roadside markets, which offer an abundance of local dishes for takeaway or casual dining. These meals pair naturally with the area's outdoor pursuits: hikes around Dewa Sanzan, the sacred trio of mountains representing the stages of life. While completing all three peaks is a multi-day journey, Mount Haguro can be climbed in a day, with mountain inns offering quiet refuge along the trail.

YAMAGATA PREFECTURE

Yonezawa Station, Yamagata・米沢駅、山形県

37.9095° N, 140.1283° E

GYUNIKU DOMANNAKA

Beef Domannaka・牛肉どまん中

Consistently ranked among Japan's best ekiben, Gyuniku Domannaka takes its name from Domannaka rice, a variety developed in Yamagata. The rice is prized for its light texture and remarkable ability to remain soft even after cooling – an essential quality for ekiben.

Created in Yonezawa in 1993, this bento is an evolution of the company's earlier beef sukiyaki bento, refined to better suit travel. Two styles of braised beef crown the signature rice: one thinly sliced, the other roughly minced, offering contrasting textures within a single box. The beef is seasoned with Yamagata soy sauce, which is richer and more well rounded than standard soy sauces, giving the dish a depth that sets it apart from other gyudon-style (beef and rice bowl) meals. Its popularity has led to numerous variations over the years, including versions seasoned with miso, salt or curry.

Opening the lid

1. GYU SOBORO TO GYUNIKU-NI (PAGE 80)

Minced beef and thinly sliced braised beef, cooked separately to highlight their differing textures while sharing the same savoury-sweet seasoning.

2. NISHIN KOMBU MAKI

Dried herring wrapped in kombu and tied with kanpyo (dried gourd strips), then gently braised. Likely introduced via Hokkaido trade routes, it has a mild, sardine-like flavour that is softened by the tender seaweed which is wrapped around the fish.

3. NIMONO (PAGE 29)

Braised carrot and potato, providing gentle sweetness alongside the beef.

4. KAMABOKO

A soft fish cake with a consistency similar to mochi.

5. DASHIMAKI TAMAGO (PAGE 26)

Rolled omelette seasoned with dashi.

6. GARI

Pickled ginger to refresh the palate.

RECIPES ➡

GYU SOBORO TO GYUNIKU-NI

Serves 2

MINCED BEEF AND BRAISED BEEF・牛そぼろと牛肉煮

This dish combines sliced beef and beef mince, though either can be used exclusively if preferred. The flavours are reminiscent of the gyudon (thin slices of beef stewed in sweetened soy, mirin and sake, served over rice) found at chain restaurants, making it an ideal topping to serve simply over rice. An onsen tamago (soft-boiled egg, page 137) is a natural accompaniment.

- 1 tablespoon neutral oil
- 150 g (5½ oz) beef, sliced about 3 mm (⅛ in) thick against the grain (see Note)
- 150 g (5½ oz) minced (ground) beef
- 100 ml (3½ fl oz) sake
- 30 ml (1 fl oz) mirin
- 70 ml (2¼ fl oz) soy sauce
- 1 tablespoon zarame or caster (superfine) sugar
- 1 teaspoon grated ginger
- steamed rice (page 22), to serve

Heat a saucepan over medium heat and add the oil.

Add the sliced and minced beef, keeping them on separate sides of the pan, and stir-fry for 3–5 minutes, until lightly coloured.

Add the sake, mirin, soy sauce, zarame and ginger. Bring to the boil, skim off any scum, then reduce the heat and simmer for 5–10 minutes, until the beef is tender and the sauce has reduced slightly.

Remove from the heat. Spoon the minced and sliced beef over rice, keeping them divided so their contrasting textures can be enjoyed.

This dish can be enjoyed hot or cold, and will keep in the fridge for up to 3 days.

NOTE //

A flavourful secondary cut is preferable to premium steaks such as sirloin or ribeye. Beef chuck is an excellent and economical choice.

THROUGH MOUNTAINS & FIELDS

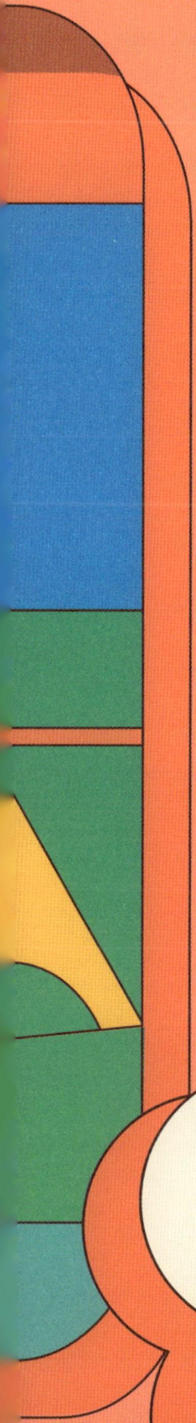

MID JAPAN

·

From Niigata
to Himeji

The mountains loosen their grip, and the landscape begins to open. Rivers widen, fields flatten, and the train gathers speed. This is a stretch defined by movement and exchange – grain and vegetables flowing out of valleys, people and ideas moving steadily towards the big cities.

Niigata's rice fields give way to Toyama's coast and the long reach of the Hokuriku line, where seafood arrives fresh and early, and meals remain tethered to the day's catch. But the sense of distance begins to shorten. Stations come more frequently now, timetables tighten, and food becomes less about endurance and more about balance.

Before Tokyo appears, you feel it: the density of tracks, the layering of lines, the quiet choreography of transfers. Here, ekiben are no longer provisions against isolation but companions to motion. Ingredients from across the country converge – rice from the north, fish from distant coasts, pickles perfected elsewhere and shipped to the capital.

Yokohama carries the sea back into the picture, its port long open to outside influence. Western techniques, Chinese seasonings and a taste for novelty sit easily alongside older traditions. Bentos here feel cosmopolitan: sandwiches sit alongside shumai, flavours are less bound to a single place, reflecting a city shaped by arrival and departure over centuries.

As the train continues west, through Shizuoka and Aichi, fields reappear, factories edge closer to the tracks, and food becomes practical once more. Tea from Shizuoka, miso and eel from Aichi: flavours deepen and bolden, asserting identity amid constant movement.

Approaching the Kansai region, the tone shifts decisively. There is a confidence to the food as the train passes the old capitals of Kyoto and Nara, whose kitchens have fed Japan for centuries. The flavours are bold, generous and familiar, shaped equally by refinement and everyday appetite. It is a cuisine with a clear identity, formed where modernity and memory meet.

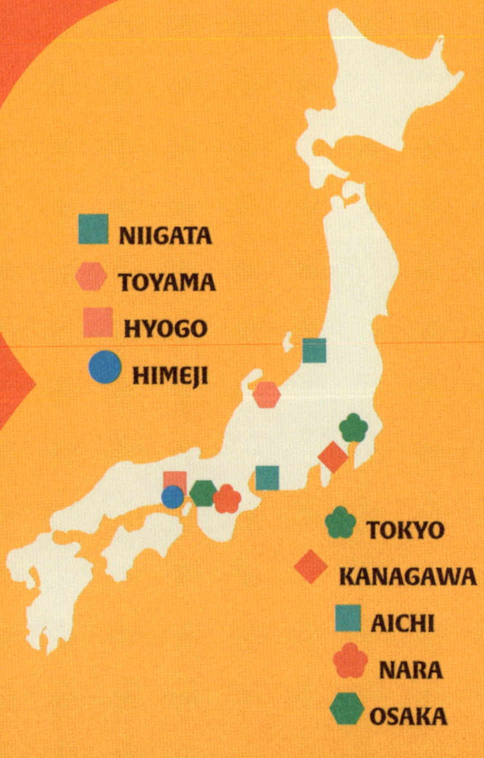

NIIGATA

Facing the Sea of Japan, Niigata is a region defined by rice, sake and seafood. Its celebrated Koshihikari rice forms the backbone of local cuisine, prized for its natural sweetness, gentle stickiness and clean finish. Alongside it is Niigata's tanrei karakuchi sake – crisp, dry and refreshing, designed to cleanse the palate and pair seamlessly with food.

The surrounding waters yield an abundance of seafood: sweet prawns (shrimp), tender squid, snow crab and white shrimp appear regularly in local cooking. Inland, the region is also known for distinctive dishes rarely found elsewhere, such as hegi soba, made with funori seaweed. The seaweed gives the soba noodles a slippery, elastic texture and a subtle marine note. Served in rectangular wooden trays, hegi soba is prized for its springiness.

From premium rice and pristine seafood to subtle, region-specific preparations, Niigata's cuisine favours balance and clean flavours over excess. It is a food culture built on seasonality and precision – a reflection of the land, the sea, and the skill of those who work them.

NIIGATA PREFECTURE

Niigata Station, Niigata・新潟駅、新潟県

37.9120° N, 139.0614° E

EBI SENRYO CHIRASHI

Senryo prawn chirashi・えび千両ちらし

Senryo is the name of a premium restaurant chain in Japan, and its name carries a connotation of great value or wealth. 'Sen' means thousand and 'ryo' was a unit of gold in pre-Meiji Restoration Japan. The illustration on the lid offers only a hint of what lies hidden below, inviting the eater to uncover its contents.

Unlike most ekiben, where ingredients are displayed openly, this bento conceals its riches beneath a thick blanket of dashi-flavoured tamago (rolled omelette, page 26), scattered with fine flakes of cooked prawns (shrimp). Beneath the omelette are layers of carefully prepared seafood: toothsome squid, plump vinegared prawns, eel glazed in kabayaki sauce, and kohada (gizzard shad) which has been cured in salt and vinegar and finished with wasabi and soy. Everything rests on a layer of oboro kombu – paper-thin shaved kombu that nearly melts on the tongue, leaving behind a lingering umami sensation.

With its substantially sized omelette and generous portion of seafood, this is an eye-catching and filling ekiben, well suited to long Shinkansen journeys. The lid itself doubles as a postcard, a thoughtful and distinctive detail unique to this bento.

Opening the lid

1. EBI
Large, sweet prawns (shrimp), which have been simply boiled with a touch of white vinegar.

2. UNAGI (PAGE 132)
Thick-cut river eel cooked in kabayaki sauce, rich and glossy from soy, mirin and sake reduced with eel bones.

3. KOHADA
Gizzard shad, a prized silver-skinned fish rarely seen in ekiben due to its cost, short shelf life, and exacting preparation. Firmer and more delicate than mackerel, it is cured in salt and vinegar and finished with wasabi soy and pickled ginger.

4. IKA
Boiled squid, tender yet pleasantly firm.

5. DASHIMAKI TAMAGO (PAGE 26)
A thick omelette sheet blankets the bento, concealing the seafood below.

6. EBI OBORO
Finely crumbled cooked prawn scattered over the omelette, adding flavour and an auspicious pink accent.

TOYAMA

Toyama lies between the Northern Alps and the Sea of Japan, a geography that shapes both what people eat and how they cook. Snowmelt from the mountains feeds rivers and rice fields before flowing directly into Toyama Bay, creating one of Japan's most productive fishing grounds.

Firefly squid, white prawns (shrimp), yellowtail and trout are abundant in these waters and are treated with restraint in the ways they are cooked. Boiling, curing or simply serving raw are the most common cooking techniques – allowing freshness and the seafood's natural texture to lead. Rice, nourished by cold winters and the prefecture's pure water, underpins daily meals and is valued as much for its quality as for its role alongside seafood.

Toyama's food culture favours practicality over display. Dishes are designed to travel well, sustain people through long winters, and reflect their environment. It is a cuisine that feels grounded, deeply tied to the land and sea from which it comes.

TOYAMA PREFECTURE

Toyama Station, Toyama · 富山駅、富山県

36.7021° N, 137.2126° E

MASU NO SUSHI

Trout sushi · ますのすし

Trout is rarely seen in sushi, especially the popular Edomae sushi variety, but Masu No Sushi is the notable exception. In this Toyama specialty, salt-cured trout is pressed over vinegared rice and wrapped tightly in bamboo leaves. A knife is included in the ekiben – unlike most sushi, this is intended to be sliced before eating, much like a cake.

Masu No Sushi was created in 1912 at Minamoto, a local ryokan, and was among the first ekiben sold at the newly opened Toyama Station. It is still presented in a magewappa (a traditional oval or round steam-bent cedar box) and pressed into shape, though modern versions are secured with rubber bands rather than rattan vines. Historically, the pressing served a practical purpose: preserving the fish by eliminating air, and lending the trout a gentle vinegared flavour from its prolonged contact with the rice. Today, the technique remains largely ceremonial, a link to the dish's origins.

The flavour is mild and lightly salty. Substantial in size, this is an ekiben best shared among three or four people, ideally alongside lighter dishes, such as pickles and soups.

Opening the lid

1. MASU

Local trout, thinly sliced then salted. After the salt has penetrated the fish, it is rinsed in rice vinegar. The trout has a clean, oceanic flavour, which is lightly scented with bamboo.

2. SASA

Bamboo leaves tightly wrap the trout and rice, gently perfuming them. The bamboo leaves also preserve the contents and prevent the rice and fish from sticking to the wooden container. To eat, turn the Masu No Sushi out onto its lid, then cut through the bamboo leaf wrapper to divide it into 8 wedges. Using your hands, you can peel the bamboo leaf back and enjoy using your hands or chopsticks.

3. MAGEWAPPA

The traditional packaging for the Masu No Sushi is light and strong. Bentos are stacked on top of each other, then a stone is placed on top, pushing out air to help to preserve the fish and rice, and compressing the layers, so the flavours meld together.

ITでオフィスを
元気にする
チンコ
スパス
日拓
パチンコ
エスパス
日拓
カラオケ
まねきねこ
隣のビル
4F
プロミス
プロミス
九段下 市ケ谷
Kudanshita Ichigaya
新宿駅東口
Alpen
Outdoors
ノンステップバス

TOKYO

As the hub of Japan's rail network and one of the world's most populous cities, Tokyo is often the starting point for Shinkansen journeys. There is little left to say that hasn't already been written about the city, but Tokyo Station itself remains an essential stop for ekiben lovers.

Here, in what is often considered the birthplace of ekiben culture, you encounter its full arc. There are echoes of the earliest boxes – simple, practical meals shaped by the rhythms of travel – alongside refined expressions influenced by ryokan traditions. Establishments such as Nihonbashi Daimasu adapt their osechi (elaborate year-end boxes) techniques into carefully composed bento. You'll also find icons of the modern era, like the chikin bento, a reminder of a time when chicken itself was considered a luxury.

At the same time, modern tastes and trends are on display in Tokyo's ekiben: collaborations with anime and manga brands abound, and increasingly premium ekiben featuring ingredients such as wagyu beef, uni (sea urchin) and produce sourced from across the country are common. Tokyo does not erase regional food so much as collect and refine it. If you're lucky, you'll find the Aomori Hitokuchi Darake, an ekiben with 24 different bites showcasing Aomori's produce. An extreme example of how elaborate ekiben can become.

Just beyond the ticket gates at Tokyo Station is Ekiben Matsuri (page 74), a store bringing together bentos from across the country. The selection rotates frequently, so if something catches your eye, it's best to buy it immediately – it may be gone when you return.

TOKYO

Tokyo Station, Tokyo · 東京駅、東京都

35.6826° N, 139.7648° E

CHIKIN BENTO

Chicken bento · チキン弁当

Introduced in 1964 alongside the opening of the Tokaido Shinkansen, Chikin Bento was once considered a premium offering. Priced at 45 yen (when most bentos sold for around 40) it reflected a time when chicken itself was still regarded as a luxury ingredient. Today, Chikin Bento is an inexpensive and deeply nostalgic ekiben, fondly beloved and remembered by children and adults alike.

The contents are deliberately simple: tomato ketchup-flavoured rice with peas, karaage chicken, a small salad and a pouch of lemon juice. What elevates this bento are the small details – a stick of smoked cheese, soft scrambled egg, and a sun-dried tomato that intensifies the sweetness of the ketchup rice. Even the salad has evolved over time, shifting from macaroni salad to the current mix of lightly pickled carrot, cabbage and beetroot (beets).

Look closely at the chopstick wrapper and you'll find two mascots: the original 1964 chicken on one side, and a more modern version on the other – a subtle visual record of how the bento has changed with the times.

Opening the lid

1. KARAAGE (PAGE 98)

Japan's beloved fried chicken, marinated in soy and ginger, coated in potato starch, and fried until juicy and crisp. The ekiben also comes with a small pouch of lemon juice to brighten the dish.

2. KETCHUP RICE (PAGE 99)

A family favourite of rice stir-fried with ketchup, here deepened with sun-dried tomato. Finished with peas for freshness, scrambled egg for richness and sun-dried tomato for sweetness.

3. SALAD

A small mix of cabbage, red cabbage and beetroot (beets), adding colour, texture and balance to the ekiben.

4. SMOKED CHEESE

One of the bento's defining elements. Once considered a luxury ingredient, it can be eaten as is or broken over the rice.

RECIPES ➡

CHICKEN KARAAGE

Serves 2

FRIED CHICKEN・チキン唐揚げ

Perhaps the most familiar form of Japanese fried chicken, karaage is found everywhere in Japan, from convenience stores to izakaya and festival stalls. The defining feature is its light potato starch coating, which creates a delicate crust that allows the flavour of the chicken to remain prominent. Karaage is also notably good when eaten cold, as the coating will soften without becoming doughy, making it ideal for bento.

For a gluten-free version, coat the chicken exclusively with potato starch and use gluten-free soy sauce in the marinade.

200 g (7 oz) boneless, skinless chicken thighs
neutral oil, for deep-frying
150 g (5½ oz) potato starch
75 g (½ cup) plain (all-purpose) flour
salt and ground black pepper

MARINADE

2 tablespoons soy sauce
2 tablespoons sake
½ tablespoon grated ginger
1 teaspoon caster (superfine) sugar
1 teaspoon salt
½ teaspoon toasted sesame oil

In a bowl, mix together all of the marinade ingredients. Using the tip of a sharp knife, pierce each chicken thigh 8–10 times to help the marinade penetrate. Cut the chicken into bite-sized pieces and transfer to the bowl with the marinade. Cover and marinate in the fridge for 30 minutes to 1 hour.

In a heavy-based saucepan, heat about 5 cm (2 in) of oil to 165°C (330°F).

Drain the chicken and pat dry. Mix the potato starch and flour, season lightly, then coat the chicken, shaking off the excess. Fry the chicken for 2 minutes, working in batches if needed. Remove from the oil and drain on a wire rack.

Increase the oil temperature to 180°C (350°F) and fry the chicken again for a further 2 minutes, or until a skewer inserted into the centre feels hot.

Drain briefly on a wire rack. Serve warm, or allow to cool, then refrigerate and serve cold the next day or reheated in a microwave for 1 minute.

KETCHUP RICE

Serves 2

ケチャップライス

The ketchup rice in Tokyo's Chikin Bento is plain, without added vegetables cooked into the rice, and only a scattering of peas on top. This version includes ingredients commonly found in ketchup rice to add texture and nutrition, but they can be omitted if preferred.

Instead of the rice, you could also use 200 g (7 oz) cooked spaghetti, to make spaghetti napolitan, another favourite Japanese fusion dish.

- 2 tablespoons tomato ketchup
- 2 teaspoons soy sauce
- 3 tablespoons neutral oil
- ½ onion, diced into 1 cm (½ in) pieces
- ½ bell pepper (capsicum), diced
- 4 button mushrooms, sliced
- 1 tablespoon frozen peas
- 2 tablespoons diced ham
- 370 g (2 cups) cooked short-grain white rice, cooled
- 2 eggs
- 1 tablespoon chopped sun-dried tomato

In a small bowl, mix together the ketchup and soy sauce.

Heat 2 tablespoons of the oil in a large frying pan and stir-fry the onion, bell pepper, mushroom, peas and ham over medium heat for about 5 minutes, until the onion softens.

Add the rice and warm through, then stir in the soy sauce and ketchup mixture. Cook for another 5 minutes, or until the ketchup and soy sauce have been absorbed into the rice.

Whisk the eggs until smooth. In a separate non-stick pan, heat the remaining 1 tablespoon of oil over medium heat. Add the egg, reduce the heat to low and stir constantly for about 30 seconds, until softly set.

Serve the scrambled egg over the rice and finish sprinkled with the sun-dried tomato.

The ketchup rice will keep in the fridge for up to 2 days.

駅弁
株式会社
関根屋
クレヨンしんちゃんのお弁当
クレヨンしんちゃん
家族都市
秋田県

KYARA BEN • CHARACTER BENTO
キャラ弁

If there's a popular character in Japan, you'll probably find it on an ekiben. From classics like Anpanman and Crayon Shin-chan to recent favourites like Pikmin and Kuromi, character-themed bento are everywhere. Some come in boxes shaped like the character's silhouette, others feature their faces rendered in food.

These bentos blend regional food traditions with beloved characters from anime, manga and local tourism campaigns. Trains themselves are a frequent motif: Shinkansen, historic locomotives and even shipping containers are recreated as ekiben boxes. Their appeal lies not only in the flavours but also in the playful presentation: colourful boxes, bespoke wrappings, and rice or side dishes shaped to evoke the featured character. For families, collectors and travellers, they offer a sense of novelty and delight that stands apart from more traditional ekiben.

The contents are usually crowd-pleasers – hamburg steak, panko-crumbed prawn (shrimp), frankfurter, ketchup rice and other favourites. Some boxes also highlight a character's origin or connection to a region. For example, Crayon Shin-chan's ekiben is produced by an Akita-based maker (Akita being the hometown of Shin-chan's father, Hiroshi), and includes the local ingredient tonburi (cypress seeds) inside a fish cake. Kumamoto mascot, Kumamon, has a bento featuring hirai chikuwa salad tempura – potato salad stuffed into fish paste cake and deep-fried – as well as ikinari dango, a sweet dumpling filled with sweet potato and red beans.

Anime-based ekiben have also surged in popularity. Series like *Demon Slayer* offer character-inspired bento designed to reflect personality traits. Tanjiro's earnest nature and rural origins are expressed through simple roast pork, abundant vegetables, and subtly flavoured items like candied chestnuts and apricots. Inosuke's brashness, by contrast, is represented with two oversized tempura prawns (shrimp) – echoing his dual-sword fighting style – and richer bolder flavours such as tempura-braised pork and burdock.

While some of these bento can be found in major cities, many are sold only in specific regions. This exclusivity encourages travellers to seek them out, blending tourism, local pride and pop culture into a uniquely Japanese experience.

TOKYO

Tokyo Station, Tokyo・東京駅、東京都

35.6826° N, 139.7648° E

TAKENOKO GOHAN ORIZUME

Bamboo shoot rice orizume・たけのこごはん折詰

This seasonal bento from the department store Nihonbashi Daimasu (founded in 1900) is a clear expression of Japan's deep respect for seasonality. In autumn, chestnuts dominate; winter brings shellfish such as scallops and oysters; spring highlights wild mountain vegetables. This spring and early summer offering centres on bamboo shoots – a classic marker of warmer months and new growth.

A variety of small dishes celebrates spring and early summer abundance: peas, beans, clams and vegetables appear throughout both layers of this ekiben, finishing with a chewy, mochi-like dessert that has been flavoured with mugwort (an aromatic herb known for its bitter taste) and filled with sweet red bean paste.

The word 'orizume' in the ekiben's name refers to the packaging itself – a thin, neatly crafted wooden box traditionally used for theatre outings, picnics and special bentos. This ekiben is also presented in two tiers, once considered a mark of luxury. While premium bentos today often come in single layers, the double-tier format retains a sense of occasion.

Opening the lid

1. TAKENOKO GOHAN (PAGE 104)

Fresh bamboo shoots are abundant in spring and early summer, they are poached simply and sit on a bed of rice that has been cooked in the liquid that was used to braise the bamboo shoots, absorbing their gentle sweetness and earthy aroma. Green peas and a carrot cut into a sakura (cherry blossom) shape reinforce the ekiben's seasonality.

2. SAWARA NO YUZU SAIKYO-YAKI (PAGE 105)

Spanish mackerel marinated in yuzu, soy and saikyo miso, then grilled. Bright citrus notes balance the natural richness of the fish.

3. ASARINI

Vegetables, such as carrot and komatsuna (Japanese mustard greens), gently braised with clams, giving a light seafood flavour well suited to warmer months.

4. KIRIKOMBU NI

Thinly shredded kombu stir-fried with carrot, then simmered, resulting in a crunchy, salad-like side dish.

5. KAMABOKO

Fish balls mixed with kikurage (wood ear mushroom), combining bounce and crunch.

6. TSUKUNE (PAGE 106)

Chicken meatballs containing chopped cartilage for a pleasing crunch, topped with fuki miso (page 107). Lighter than the usual sweet soy glaze, this version feels fresh and delicate.

7. DASHIMAKI TAMAGO (PAGE 26)

A slice of softly set dashimaki tamago.

8. EDO UMANI

A home-style dish dating back to the Edo period, where meat, seafood and vegetables are simmered together in a sweet soy-based sauce. The shared cooking symbolises wishes for family unity and prosperity. Here it features pumpkin (winter squash), carrot, green beans, burdock root and ganmodoki (fried tofu mixed with vegetables).

9. KONNYAKU

Thick-cut konnyaku (konjac yam) gently simmered in dashi, mildly flavoured with a springy texture.

10. YOMOGI MANJU (PAGE 107)

A small steamed bun that has been flavoured with yomogi (mugwort) and filled with red bean paste. Chewy and gently sweet, with a texture similar to mochi.

RECIPES ➡

TAKENOKO GOHAN

Serves 4

BAMBOO SHOOT RICE・たけのこご飯

Fresh bamboo shoots are a defining flavour of spring and early summer in many parts of Japan, including Tokyo. While freshly dug shoots are ideal for this dish, they are not easily accessible outside of Japan. Frozen or vacuum-packed bamboo shoots are a practical substitute and work well in this preparation.

- 2 pieces abura-age (fried tofu pockets)
- 1 whole cooked bamboo shoot (tinned or vacuum-packed), about 100 g (3½ oz), drained
- 500 ml (2 cups) dashi (page 23)
- 2 tablespoons mirin
- 2 tablespoons sake
- 2 tablespoons soy sauce
- 1 tablespoon caster (superfine) sugar
- 300 g (10½ oz) short-grain white rice

Bring a saucepan of water to the boil and blanch the abura-age for about 2 minutes. Drain, then squeeze out the excess water.

Cut the bamboo shoot in half and place in a saucepan with the dashi. Bring to a simmer over medium heat.

After about 15 minutes, once the bamboo shoot has slightly softened, add the blanched abura-age, mirin, sake, soy sauce and sugar. Cover with a cartouche (a round of baking paper with a small hole cut in the centre) and simmer for a further 15 minutes.

Remove from the heat and allow to cool. Reserve the braising liquid and slice the cooled bamboo shoot into thin wedges. Cut the abura-age into small squares.

Wash the rice until the water runs clear.

Add the washed rice to a donabe, lidded saucepan or rice cooker along with about 350 ml (12 fl oz) of the braising liquid (or enough liquid to reach the level recommended by the rice cooker manufacturer). Follow the instructions on page 22 to soak and cook the rice.

Serve the rice either with the bamboo shoot and abura-age arranged on top, or mixed through.

The bamboo shoot rice will keep in the fridge for up to 3 days.

SAWARA NO YUZU SAIKYO-YAKI

Serves 4

GRILLED SPANISH MACKEREL WITH YUZU AND SAIKYO MISO • 鰆の柚子西京焼き

Sawara, or Spanish mackerel, is a very common fish in Japan. Here it has been gently marinated in sweet Kyoto-style saikyo miso, which is lightly scented with yuzu, then grilled until just cooked. The miso's mild sweetness and the citrus perfume of yuzu highlight the fish's clean, delicate flavour, while the sugars in the miso and soy develop a soft, glossy sheen as it grills.

This is a restrained, time-honoured preparation that works just as well for other types of fish, such as cod or trout.

1 tablespoon salt

4 × 50 g (1¾ oz) Spanish mackerel fillets

MARINADE

125 ml (½ cup) sake

80 ml (⅓ cup) mirin

40 ml (1¼ fl oz) soy sauce

80 g (2¾ oz) saikyo miso (sweet white miso paste)

20 ml (¾ fl oz) yuzu juice

juice and peel of ½ lemon

Dissolve the salt in 500 ml (2 cups) water. Rinse the mackerel in the salted water, then drain and pat dry with paper towel. (This step helps remove any excess 'fishiness.')

To make the marinade, bring the sake and mirin to the boil in a small saucepan and cook for 1 minute to reduce the alcohol.

Remove from the heat and whisk in the soy sauce and miso until smooth. Add the yuzu juice, then squeeze in the lemon juice and add the lemon peel as well. Refrigerate or chill on ice until cold.

Place half the marinade in a container, then add the fish in a single layer. Cover with the remaining marinade. Lay paper towel directly on top, then cover with plastic wrap and refrigerate overnight.

The next day, remove the paper towel, scrape the marinade off the fish and pat the fish dry with paper towel. Allow the fish to come to room temperature for 20 minutes before cooking.

Set your oven grill (broiler) to high. Once heated, grill the fish for 8–10 minutes, watching carefully, until lightly charred and just cooked through.

Enjoy straight away, or keep in the fridge for up to 2 days.

TSUKUNE

Makes 12

CHICKEN MEATBALLS・つくね

Plump chicken meatballs are regular accompaniments to ekiben. The inclusion of tofu makes the texture soft, while the chopped chicken cartilage adds crunch. I've included a recipe for yakitori tare, a sweet sauce that's commonly used to baste tsukune and other grilled chicken – but you can also serve the meatballs with only the fuki miso, as the ekiben does.

- 100 g (3½ oz) onion
- 250 g (9 oz) minced (ground) chicken (thigh preferred)
- 25 g (1 oz) chicken cartilage (see Notes), finely chopped
- 1 egg white
- 25 g (1 oz) silken tofu
- 1 tablespoon salt
- ½ teaspoon ground black pepper
- 125 ml (½ cup) yakitori tare (optional; see below)
- fuki miso (opposite), to serve

YAKITORI TARE

- 75 ml (2½ fl oz) soy sauce
- 75 ml (2½ fl oz) mirin
- 25 ml (¾ fl oz) sake
- 50 g (1¾ oz) raw sugar
- 2 spring onions (scallions), green part only

To make the yakitori tare, mix the soy sauce, mirin, sake and sugar in a small saucepan and simmer for about 10 minutes, until reduced by one-quarter. Add the spring onion and simmer for 10 minutes more. Strain, then leave to cool. The yakitori tare will keep in the fridge for up to 1 month, and makes about 125 ml (½ cup).

To make the meatballs, finely mince the onion with a knife, rinse in cold water three times, then drain and dry.

Place the onion in a bowl with the chicken, cartilage, egg white, tofu, salt and pepper. Mix together until sticky and well combined. Form into 12 meatballs, using a large spoon to scoop out and shape the mixture.

Bring a saucepan of water to a gentle simmer. Add the meatballs and gently poach for 3 minutes. Drain and leave to cool. Once poached, the meatballs can be refrigerated overnight if preparing ahead.

Grill or pan-fry the meatballs over medium-high heat for 5–6 minutes, until browned all over.

To finish the meatballs, brush them on both sides with the yakitori tare and grill or pan-fry for another 3–4 minutes, until the coating is caramelised, or simply serve the meatballs topped with a teaspoon of fuki miso.

Once grilled, the meatballs keep in the fridge for up to 3 days.

NOTES //

Chicken cartilage can be purchased from a butcher or an Asian grocers.

In the Nihonbashi Daimasu ekiben, the meatballs are deep-fried, rather than grilled, as in the recipe above. If you prefer, you can deep-fry your tsukune too – just omit the poaching step and fry them directly in oil at 160°C (320°F) for 5 minutes.

FUKI MISO

BUTTERBUR MISO・蕗味噌

Makes about 60 ml (¼ cup)

Fuki (also called butterbur) is a stalk vegetable that is native to Japan, it has a unique fragrance and is known for its earthy, slightly bitter flavour. Fuki can be difficult to source outside Japan, celery leaves provide a suitable substitute.

This miso is used to top the tsukune (opposite), but it is an adaptable side sauce for a number of grilled meat and fish.

- ¼ cup celery leaves
- 50 g (1¾ oz) shiro miso (white miso paste)
- 1 tablespoon mirin
- 1 teaspoon rice vinegar
- 1 teaspoon caster (superfine) sugar
- ½ teaspoon mustard powder

Using a mortar and pestle, grind the celery leaves to a paste, then mix with the remaining ingredients.

This miso is best enjoyed within 24 hours.

KUSAMOCHI

MUGWORT MOCHI・草餅

Makes 6

The Nihonbashi Daimasu ekiben includes a dessert called yomogi manju, which is very similar to mochi, so I have included a recipe for kusamochi here.

Kusamochi translates to 'herb mochi'; it uses dried yomogi (mugwort) powder in place of fresh mugwort leaves, lending a subtle herbal aroma and pale green hue. It can be omitted or replaced with matcha or other powdered flavourings, depending on your preference.

- 1 tablespoon yomogi powder
- 85 g (3 oz) joshinko (non-glutinous rice flour)
- 15 g (½ oz) shiratamako (glutinous rice flour)
- 130 ml (4½ fl oz) lukewarm water
- 1 tablespoon caster (superfine) sugar
- ½ teaspoon salt
- potato starch, for dusting
- 150 g (5½ oz) red bean paste, divided into 6 balls

In a bowl, mix the yomogi powder with 1 tablespoon hot water.

In a separate microwave-safe bowl, mix the flours together. Gradually mix in the lukewarm water, then incorporate the yomogi paste, sugar and salt.

Cover and microwave at 500W for 2 minutes. Stir the mixture, then cover and cook for a further 2 minutes, until smooth and no flour patches remain.

Dust a work surface with potato starch, place the dough on top and dust again. Roll the dough out to a rectangle measuring about 24 cm × 16 cm (9½ × 6¼ in). Cut into six 8 cm (3¼ in) squares.

Place a ball of red bean paste in the centre of each square and bring in the sides to enclose. Twist the ends to seal each mochi.

Store in an airtight container for up to 24 hours.

鎌倉
KAMAKURA
1251

KANAGAWA

Once a modest fishing village, in the mid-nineteenth century Yokohama became one of the first Japanese ports to open to the world. Foreign traders, diplomats and sailors arrived in waves, bringing new ingredients, techniques and tastes. Bakeries, beer halls and Western-style cafes appeared alongside soy sauce warehouses and noodle stalls. Over time, Kanagawa absorbed these influences, developing a layered food culture: Chinese dishes were adapted to Japanese palates, Western recipes have been softened by local sensibilities, and home-grown dishes that spread nationwide, such as spaghetti napolitan and gyunabe, an early ancestor of sukiyaki (Japanese hot pot).

South of Yokohama lies Kamakura, once the seat of the shogunate and now Tokyo's closest coastal retreat. Despite being less than an hour away from the capital, Kamakura feels noticeably slower and more spacious, with small shops and cafes opening onto gardens. Food here is restrained and seasonal. Shirasu – tiny whitebait – are a local specialty, they tend to be lightly boiled and served simply over rice, delicate and gently sweet.

To the west, the land rises towards Hakone. Sulphur drifts through the mountain air, and travellers have paused here for centuries – first along the Tokaido Road, later by train and ropeway. Hakone's cuisine reflects its terrain: tofu made with pure spring water; eggs cooked in volcanic steam until their shells turn black.

Kanagawa is a prefecture constantly changing, shaped by movement, trade and tide.

KANAGAWA PREFECTURE

Yokohama Station, Kanagawa ・ 横浜駅、神奈川県

35.4662° N, 139.6232° E

SHUMAI BENTO

Pork dumpling bento ・ シュウマイ弁当

Yokohama's Chinatown gave rise to this iconic bento, which has remained largely unchanged since it was first introduced in 1954 by Kiyoken, a Chinese restaurant founded in 1888.

The meal is packed in a kyogi – a thin wooden box that absorbs excess moisture, keeping both the rice and shumai (steamed pork dumplings) from becoming soggy. For those curious about its production, Kiyoken still offers factory tours where the bentos are made.

Consistently ranked among the top three best-selling ekiben in Japan, Shumai Bento owes its popularity to its affordability, variety of ingredients and instantly recognisable presentation. Few ekiben have achieved such longevity without sacrificing clarity of purpose or flavour.

Opening the lid

1. SHUMAI (PAGE 112)

Five pieces of Kiyoken's signature shumai (steamed dumplings) form the heart of the bento. Firmer than many restaurant versions, they are made primarily from finely minced pork, with dried scallop added for more depth of flavour. Designed to be eaten lukewarm or at room temperature, their flavour is enhanced with mustard (karashi) and soy sauce.

2. MAGURO-ZUKE YAKI

Tuna that has been marinated in soy and lightly grilled. The marinade gives the fish a salinity that helps it stand up to the other strong flavours. Salmon can be used in its place.

3. ANZU

A dried apricot placed at the centre of one compartment of the bento. Its sweet-yet-tart flavour cuts through the richer components.

4. TAKENOKO

Chopped braised bamboo shoots add an element of crunch and a slightly sweet flavour contrast.

5. KAMABOKO

Pink-ringed fish cake, familiar and gently sweet.

6. KARAAGE (PAGE 98)

Including a fried component, in the form of a delicious piece of chicken, shows the depth of skill of the maker, having steamed, grilled, braised and fried elements together in one bento.

7. DASHIMAKI TAMAGO (PAGE 26)

Rolled omelette brings colour and sweetness.

8. KOMBU NO TSUKUDANI

Kombu that has been simmered in soy until it is soft and richly flavoured.

9. BENISHOGA

Pickled ginger, refreshing after the richness of the shumai.

10. TAWARA GATA GOHAN

Seasoned rice shaped into small cylinders (called tawara gata), making it easy to pick up while travelling. In this bento the rice has been sprinkled with black sesame seeds.

11. UMEBOSHI

A tiny pickled plum, recalling the most traditional form of ekiben: rice with a single ume at its centre.

RECIPES ➡

SHUMAI

Makes 16

STEAMED PORK DUMPLINGS・焼売

Kiyoken's shumai often surprise first-time eaters. The filling is smooth and finely textured, rather than coarse, with the only contrast coming from peas which have been mixed directly into the filling, rather than placed on top. These shumai are slightly larger than the bite-sized versions that are in Yokohama's iconic bento, as smaller wrappers can be difficult to source.

10 g (¼ oz) dried scallops
1 tablespoon peas, fresh or frozen
½ onion
2 teaspoons potato starch
1 cm (½ in) piece ginger
250 g (9 oz) very finely minced (ground) pork
1 tablespoon pork lard
1 teaspoon caster (superfine) sugar
1 teaspoon sesame oil
½ teaspoon salt
½ teaspoon chicken stock powder (optional)
¼ teaspoon white pepper
16 round gyoza wrappers, 8 cm (3¼ in) in size
hot mustard and soy sauce, to serve

Rehydrate the dried scallops in 50 ml (1¾ fl oz) hot water for 1 hour.

Meanwhile, blanch the peas briefly, then drain. Chop the peas to make them slightly smaller and set aside.

Mince the onion very finely with a knife, rinse twice in cold water, then drain well and mix with the potato starch.

Peel and grate the ginger. Place in a clean muslin cloth, then squeeze the juice into a large bowl, discarding the pulp.

Drain the scallops, reserving 3 teaspoons of the soaking liquid. Shred the scallops, then chop roughly and add to the ginger juice, along with the reserved scallop soaking liquid.

Add the onion, pork, lard, sugar, sesame oil, salt, stock powder (if using) and pepper. Mix until sticky and well combined. Gently fold in the peas. Cover and refrigerate for 30 minutes.

Line a large bamboo steamer with baking paper.

To make the shumai, place a gyoza wrapper in your hand and spread an even layer of filling over it, using a knife. Gather the wrapper around the filling, so that the dumpling resembles an open cup with sides. Use your knife to smooth the top.

Gently press the dumpling onto the baking paper to form a flat base. Repeat with the remaining wrappers and filling.

Fill a large saucepan with water and bring to the boil over medium heat, then place the steamer with the dumplings on top.

Steam the dumplings for 10 minutes. You might need to do these in batches depending on the size of your steamer.

Serve hot, slightly warm, or at room temperature. The flavour develops as the shumai cool.

Refrigerated, they will keep for up to 3 days.

Serve in the Kiyoken style, with hot mustard and a little soy sauce on the side.

KANAGAWA PREFECTURE

Odawara Station, Kanagawa • 小田原駅、神奈川県

35.2565° N, 139.1564° E

TAIMESHI

Sea bream rice • 鯛めし

First sold at Kozu Station in 1907, Taimeshi is one of the longest-running ekiben still in existence, as it is consistently ranked among Japan's top ten. Its distinctive octagonal container has remained largely unchanged since the Showa era. Inside is brown rice that has been generously topped with pale sea bream oboro (flakes). It's accompanied by yuzu-pickled daikon, umeboshi, wasabi pickles, clams simmered in soy, kamaboko and chikuwa (two types of fish cakes). A spoon is included alongside disposable chopsticks – a practical addition for a bento that has been packed tightly to the brim.

The crumbly rice and fish flakes are not the easiest to eat, but this abundance is part of the appeal. More than a convenient meal, Taimeshi feels like a time capsule, evoking the flavours and textures of railway dining from the Meiji through to the Showa period. Even the fish cakes speak to place: Odawara has long been a centre of kamaboko production, supplying the Tokaido corridor for generations.

Originally, this bento was made using sea bream caught in Sagami Bay. When prices rose sharply in the 1960s, substitutions were used to recreate the same flavour and texture, and for a time sea bream disappeared from the filling altogether. Today, red sea bream has returned, mixed back into the oboro, restoring the dish's original character.

While the bento is associated with the city of Odawara and its station, the flavours of the bento resonate strongly with the neighbouring city of Shizuoka. The use of wasabi pickles and the restrained seafood preparation reflects the culinary sensibilities of the Tokaido region as a whole – a coastal culture shaped by fishing ports, preservation, and food made to travel.

Opening the lid

1. TAI NO OBORO (PAGE 117)

Finely flaked sea bream blankets a base of brown rice, creating an austere, almost monochrome surface. 'Oboro' literally translates to 'hazy' or 'cloud-like', reflecting the lightness of the preparation. Subtle but far from plain, it is lightly fishy, sweet and gently salted, allowing the harmony of rice and fish to take centre stage.

2. ASARI NO TSUKUDANI (PAGE 41)

Clams that have been gently simmered in soy, lending chewiness and depth to the ekiben.

3. CHIKUWA AND KAMABOKO

Grilled and steamed fish cakes with a springy, mochi-like texture. They are paired with a tartar-style sauce flavoured with wasabi stem, adding a sharp, lively contrast.

4. YUZU DAIKON

Crisp daikon that has been pickled with yuzu. The bento moves deliberately through textures – soft rice and oboro, chewy clams, bouncy fish cakes, crunchy pickles – ensuring every bite remains engaging.

5. UMEBOSHI

A small umeboshi crowns the pickles, its sweet-sour salinity acting as a final accent.

RECIPES ➡

TAI NO OBORO

Serves 4
as a rice topping

SEA BREAM FLAKES・鯛のおぼろ

Oboro is a preparation in which a protein, typically fish, shellfish or egg, is cooked while it is continuously stirred so that it eventually breaks down into fine flakes. Oboro is prized for its sweet-and-savoury flavour, which makes it a perfect topping for rice. As it is thoroughly cooked, it stores and freezes well, and makes an excellent protein option for many ekiben.

300 g (10½ oz) sea bream fillet
1½ tablespoons caster (superfine) sugar
1½ tablespoons sake
½ teaspoon salt
steamed rice (page 22), to serve
pickles, to serve

Remove the skin and bones from the fish. Wrap the fish in muslin and tie securely.

Bring a saucepan of water to the boil and simmer the wrapped fish for 5 minutes.

Carefully remove the fish, discarding the water. Once cool enough to handle, squeeze out as much moisture as possible, then massage the fish through the cloth to break it up.

Transfer the fish to a clean pan over low heat and stir constantly with chopsticks, breaking it into fine fibres.

Add the sugar, sake and salt.

Continue stirring vigorously with chopsticks for about 10 minutes so that the fish dries out completely. The oboro is ready when the fish has formed uniform, fine strands and all the liquid has evaporated. Taste and add more salt if desired.

Transfer to a tray to cool, then store in a sealed container in the fridge for up to 1 week, or freeze for up to 1 month. (If frozen, thaw before using.)

Serve over rice, with pickles on the side.

KINOKUNIYA
海老かつサンド
Cutlet Sandwich
FILLET & MINCED CUTLET SAND
GOSHADO HONTEN ORIGINAL
SAND
SINCE1898
大船軒
サンドウヰッチ
鎌倉ハム
ボンレスハム使用
KAMAKURA HAM
大船軒 サンドウヰッチ

SANDO
サンド

In 1899 at Ofuna Station in Kamakura, the first sandwich ekiben was born. Its creator, Tomioka Shuzo, had been inspired by stories from his friend Kuroda Kiyotaka – statesman, traveller, and later Japan's second prime minister (1888–1889) – who spoke fondly of the sandwiches he encountered during journeys through Europe and America. At a time when Japan was modernising rapidly and Western culture held immense fascination, a sandwich ekiben was a novelty that immediately captured the public's imagination.

This early ekiben was modest: six neat sandwich fingers – two filled with cheese, two with ham and mustard, and two combining both fillings. Yet from this humble box, the Japanese sandwich, or sando, took root. Remarkably, the original Ofuna Station sandwich is still sold today. The combination of premium Kamakura ham with mustard, mild cheese and softly sweet bread remains every bit as satisfying now as it was more than a century ago.

The katsu sando, a sandwich featuring panko-crumbed cutlets, is said to have emerged in 1931 at the katsu restaurant Isen in Tokyo. The owner devised the sandwich so that nearby geisha could enjoy katsu without risking their makeup – a clever solution that transformed a hearty dish into something portable and discreet. Originally delicate and slim, katsu sando now range from elegant tea-sandwich proportions to thick, burger-sized meals.

In this section are recipes for three of Japan's most popular sando: a prawn (shrimp) katsu sando from Kinokuniya in Kyoto (unrelated to the bookstore chain), as well as a minced-meat katsu and a pork-loin katsu from Goshado in Kumamoto, a Western-style grill founded in 1946. A five-minute walk from Kumamoto Station, Grill Goshado is famous for the sauce that accompanies their steak, and is contained in both sando. The sauce recipe is the company's secret.

Ebi katsu sando (page 120) are packed with large pieces of bouncy prawns which have been bound together with a prawn and fish paste that adds depth, sweetness and rich umami while holding the cutlet together. It's one of my personal favourites.

Menchi katsu, or mince katsu (page 122), resembles a hamburg steak (page 52) that has been transformed into a cutlet. The panko crust absorbs the sauce beautifully, keeping the bread from becoming soggy while maintaining a juicy centre. It's an ingenious creation – and can be a brilliant way to use leftover hamburg mixture.

Finally, the tonkatsu sando (page 124), often simply called 'katsu sando', features a straightforward combination of pork loin and katsu sauce. Its simplicity highlights the quality of the pork itself. When serving these cold, I prefer using thinner cuts (up to about 1.5 cm/½ in), as thicker pork cuts can firm up and become harder to bite when chilled.

EBI KATSU SANDO

海老かつサンド

Bouncy, crunchy prawns paired with tartar and tonkatsu sauce create a flavour and texture combination that's hard to beat. Despite being deep-fried, the sandwich feels clean and surprisingly light. The sweetness of the prawns comes through clearly, without being weighed down by heavy seasoning, while the sauces add richness and contrast.

Makes 4

2 tablespoons diced onion
1 tablespoon potato starch
150 g (5½ oz) prawns (shrimp), peeled and deveined
1 tablespoon sake
1½ teaspoons salt
100 g (3½ oz) hanpen (white fish paste)
2 tablespoons Japanese mayonnaise
½ teaspoon ground white pepper

FOR CRUMBING AND FRYING

50 g (⅓ cup) plain (all-purpose) flour
50 ml (1¾ fl oz) milk
1 egg
120 g (2 cups) panko breadcrumbs
neutral oil, for deep-frying

FOR ASSEMBLING THE SANDO

8 slices shokupan (page 126), about 1.5–2 cm (½–¾ in) thick
tartar sauce (page 221)
tonkatsu sauce (page 125)

To make the patties, rinse the diced onion in water and drain, then mix with the potato starch.

Place the prawns in a bowl and massage with the sake and 1 teaspoon of the salt until the water becomes cloudy. Rinse and drain.

Roughly chop the prawns, then mix with all the other patty ingredients, including the remaining ½ teaspoon salt.

Shape into four oval patties, about 1.5–2 cm (½–¾ in) thick. Lay them on a sheet of baking paper, in one layer, and freeze for 3 hours (or overnight) to set the shape. (If freezing overnight, crumb the patties while still frozen.)

To crumb the patties, in a bowl, whisk together the flour, milk and egg. Place the panko in a second bowl. Line a tray with baking paper, ready for the crumbed patties.

Crumb the patties by first coating them in the egg mixture, then coat in the panko, shaking off the excess after each coat, and placing them on the lined baking tray, ready for frying. (The patties at this point can be frozen for up to 1 month; thaw before deep-frying.)

To fry the katsu, heat about 5 cm (2 in) of oil to 180°C (350°F) in a large deep heavy-based saucepan or deep-fryer. Deep-fry the patties, in batches if needed to avoid overcrowding, for 3 minutes, or until a skewer inserted into the centre comes out hot.

Remove from the oil and place on a wire rack to drain. You can either enjoy the ebi katsu immediately, or allow them to cool to room temperature to make a sando.

To make a sando, spread one slice of bread with tartar sauce and a second slice with tonkatsu sauce. Sandwich the sauced sides together with an ebi katsu in between, then repeat with the remaining bread and ebi katsu. Wrap tightly in plastic wrap and allow to 'marinate' on a work surface for 30 minutes.

Unwrap each sando, cut off the crusts, then slice in half and serve. You can also make the sando a day in advance and keep in the fridge for lunch.

MENCHI KATSU SANDO

メンチカツサンド

While you can use the hamburg mix on page 52, this is a slightly different version that's more juicy with a different ratio of beef and pork. The higher ratio of beef to pork brings a little more flavour at the expense of tenderness, but that's offset by the addition of beef lard. The lard makes the katsu extra juicy, which is achievable because it's encased in panko; if it was cooked as a hamburger, the lard would simply melt away.

Makes 8

1 tablespoon neutral oil or beef lard
1 onion, finely diced
20 g (⅓ cup) panko breadcrumbs
60 ml (¼ cup) milk
50 g (1¾ oz) beef lard
300 g (10½ oz) minced (ground) beef
100 g (3½ oz) minced (ground) pork
½ teaspoon salt
½ teaspoon ground black pepper
½ teaspoon ground nutmeg

FOR CRUMBING AND FRYING

100 g (⅔ cup) plain (all-purpose) flour
100 ml (3½ fl oz) milk
2 eggs
120 g (2 cups) panko breadcrumbs
neutral oil, for deep-frying

FOR ASSEMBLING THE SANDO

16 slices shokupan (page 126), about 1.5–2 cm (½–¾ in) thick
tonkatsu sauce (page 125)
Japanese mayonnaise

To make the patties, heat a frying pan over medium heat. Add the oil and slowly cook the onion for 10–15 minutes, until softened and lightly browned. Remove from the pan and cool in the fridge, so it won't heat the meat when mixed into the patties.

In a small bowl, mix the panko and milk and set aside to rehydrate in the fridge while preparing other ingredients.

Warm the beef lard in the microwave or in a small saucepan over low heat until it has just melted, but not hot. Set aside.

In a large bowl, mix the beef and pork with the salt. Knead together until the mince becomes sticky.

Add the cooked onion, pepper and nutmeg, followed by the milk and panko. Mix together, then mix in the melted beef lard until incorporated.

Refrigerate for 20 minutes to chill the mixture.

Divide into eight equal portions and shape into rounds about 1 cm (½ in) thick. Lay them on a sheet of baking paper, in one layer. Freeze for 3 hours (or overnight) to set the shape and make the patties easier to crumb. (If freezing overnight, crumb the patties while still frozen.)

To crumb the patties, in a bowl, whisk together the flour, milk and eggs. Place the panko in a second bowl. Line a tray with baking paper, ready for the crumbed katsu.

Crumb the patties by first coating them in the egg mixture, then coat in the panko, shaking off the excess after each coat. Place them on the lined baking tray, ready for frying. (The patties at this point can be frozen for up to 1 month; thaw before deep-frying.)

To fry the katsu, heat about 5 cm (2 in) of oil to 180°C (350°F) in a large deep heavy-based saucepan or deep-fryer. Deep-fry the patties, in batches if needed to avoid overcrowding, for 3 minutes, or until a skewer inserted into the centre comes out hot.

Drain thoroughly on a wire rack. You can either enjoy the menchi katsu immediately, or allow them to cool to room temperature to make a sando.

To make a sando, spread one slice of bread with tonkatsu sauce and a second slice with mayonnaise. Sandwich the sauced sides together with a menchi katsu in between, then repeat with the remaining bread and patties. Wrap tightly in plastic wrap and allow to 'marinate' on a work surface for 30 minutes.

Unwrap each sando, cut off the crusts, then slice in half and serve. You can also make the sando a day in advance and keep in the fridge for lunch.

KATSU SANDO

カツサンド

The pork in Japan is different. It's tender and marbled, with fat that melts away without becoming chewy. Here's a way to give your pork tonkatsu a similar quality without flying to Japan. The key is a light brine for tenderness and juiciness, and tenderising with a knife.

Katsu sando is a classic because it relies on restraint: good pork, soft bread, and just enough sauce to bind everything together.

Serves 2

80 g (heaped ⅓ cup) caster (superfine) sugar
3 tablespoons salt
1 tablespoon whole black peppercorns
2 boneless pork loin fillets, about 1–1.5 cm (½ in) thick, fat trimmed to 5 mm (¼ in)

FOR CRUMBING AND FRYING

100 g (⅔ cup) plain (all-purpose) flour
100 ml (3½ fl oz) milk
2 eggs
120 g (2 cups) panko breadcrumbs
neutral oil, for deep-frying

FOR ASSEMBLING THE SANDO

4 slices shokupan (page 126), about 1.5–2 cm (½–¾ in) thick
tonkatsu sauce (see opposite)

To prepare the pork, in a saucepan, combine the sugar, salt, peppercorns and 1 litre (4 cups) water. Heat, stirring, until the salt and sugar dissolve, then remove from the heat and allow to cool.

Meanwhile, poke the pork all over with the point of a knife, concentrating on the fat and sinew to tenderise the meat.

When the brine is cool, add the pork and refrigerate for 2 hours.

Remove the pork from the brine, discarding the brine, and pat the pork dry with paper towel.

To crumb the cutlets, in a bowl, whisk together the flour, milk and eggs. Place the panko in a second bowl. Line a tray with baking paper.

Crumb the pork fillets by coating them in the egg mixture, then coat in the panko, shaking off the excess after each coat. Place them on the lined baking tray. (The crumbed cutlets can be frozen for up to 1 month; thaw before deep-frying.)

To fry the katsu, heat 5 cm (2 in) of oil to 170°C (340°F) in a large deep heavy-based saucepan or deep-fryer. Gently slide in the pork and cook for 3 minutes, turning halfway through. Remove the pork from the oil and test using a skewer: if the skewer comes out hot, the pork is done. Place on a wire rack and allow to rest for 2 minutes.

To make a sando, coat each slice of bread with a layer of tonkatsu sauce. Sandwich the sauced sides together with a pork katsu in between, then repeat with the remaining bread and katsu. Wrap tightly in plastic wrap and leave to 'marinate' on a work surface for 30 minutes.

Unwrap each sando, cut off the crusts, then slice in half and serve. You can also make the sando a day in advance and keep in the fridge for lunch.

TONKATSU SAUCE

とんかつソース

Makes about 250 ml (1 cup)

3 tablespoons Japanese Worcestershire sauce (see Note)
2 tablespoons tomato ketchup
1 tablespoon soy sauce
1 tablespoon Japanese mayonnaise
1 tablespoon sake
1 tablespoon dijon mustard
1 teaspoon caster (superfine) sugar

A simple tonkatsu sauce for when you can't find it in stores. It's slightly spicy from the mustard and ketchup, and rich and complex from the Japanese Worcestershire sauce and soy. You can also adjust the amount of mustard, or use a different mustard to make it more or less spicy according to your taste.

Mix all the ingredients together and serve with the sandos.

You could also make a larger quantity and keep some in the cupboard for other katsu such as beef or pork (served with rice instead of bread); the sauce is best used within 1 week.

NOTE //

Japanese Worcestershire sauce (ウスターソース) isn't like the Western variety, which is punchy, but thin and watery. The Japanese version is milder, but thicker, with more fruit. A good substitute is HP Sauce or A1 Steak Sauce, or 2 tablespoons tomato ketchup mixed with 1 tablespoon English Worcestershire sauce.

SHOKUPAN

食パン

Makes 1 loaf

220 g (8 oz) plain (all-purpose) flour, plus extra for dusting
165 ml (5½ fl oz) milk
50 g (1¾ oz) caster (superfine) sugar
10 g (1⅔ teaspoons) salt
4 g (1¼ teaspoons) dried yeast
60 g (2 oz) butter, at room temperature, diced
neutral oil, for greasing

PREFERMENT

220 g (8 oz) plain (all-purpose) flour
165 ml (5½ fl oz) water
2.5 g (¾ teaspoon) dried yeast

Japan's bread is soft, pillowy and milky, but not heavy. The balance between dairy, without oiliness, is key to a good shokupan. It should tear apart in nice long shreds too, without being too chewy. Shokupan is now common in many Asian grocery stores fresh or frozen, but it's worthwhile making your own as you can use your favourite milk and butter for a unique flavour.

You'll need one long, lidded loaf tin for this shokupan. Traditionally, Japanese bread loaf tins were measured in 'kin'. The tin used here is 1.5 kin, with external dimensions of 216 × 109 × 106 mm (8½ × 4¼ × 4⅙ in). Alternatively, use a 2.8 litre (3 qt) lidded loaf tin.

Shokupan is best when it's fresh and used in sandwiches. If it's two or more days old, toast it. Beyond 5 days, shred it up to make nama panko (fresh Japanese breadcrumbs) and store it in the freezer for crumbing tonkatsu.

To make the preferment, mix the flour, water and yeast together in bowl, then cover and leave for 24 hours at room temperature.

The next day, place the preferment in the bowl of a stand mixer. Add the flour, milk, sugar, salt and yeast and knead on low speed for 5 minutes.

Scrape down the sides of the bowl, then add the butter. Knead for 10 minutes, or until the dough is very elastic, scraping down the sides every 2 minutes.

Scrape down the side of the bowl again. Cover and leave to rest in a warm place for 1 hour, or until the dough has doubled in size.

Empty the dough out onto a clean work surface and divide into three even pieces. Shape each into a smooth ball, then cover and rest for another 20 minutes.

Lightly grease the inside of a 2.8 litre lidded loaf tin with oil.

Lightly flour your work surface. Turn one dough ball over so the smooth side faces down. Using your hands or a rolling pin, stretch the dough to roughly the size of an A4 sheet of paper.

Fold the left side of the dough over two-thirds of the dough and press down to remove any large air bubbles, then fold the right side all the way over to the left edge.

Lift the top of the dough with both hands, then tightly roll from top to bottom, to create a log. Seal the end of the roll by pinching it together, then place, seam side down, at one end of the loaf tin. Repeat with the remaining two dough balls, placing them all side by side in the tin.

Slide the lid on the loaf tin and leave in a warm place for 1 hour, or until the dough has doubled in size.

Preheat the oven to 180°C (350°F).

Place the tin in the oven for 20 minutes, then turn the oven down to 165°C (330°F) and bake the loaf for another 15 minutes.

Remove the tin from the oven, carefully remove the lid and turn the loaf out onto a wire rack.

Allow to cool for 30 minutes before slicing.

AICHI

Rice, soy and wheat form the backbone of Aichi's cuisine, supported by a long tradition of fermentation. The region is particularly known for its darker, more concentrated seasonings, which developed in part for preservation and in part to suit meals designed to be filling and sustaining. Compared to the lighter, more delicate flavours of other parts of Japan, Aichi's cooking tends towards depth and intensity, with an emphasis on umami and salinity.

Nagoya, the port city and capital of Aichi, is known for bold, deeply savoury flavours. Dark, rich hatcho miso and grilled eel are regional signatures, reflecting a food culture shaped by the area's industrial past and the need for hearty, sustaining meals.

Kishimen is a good example of the substantial meals that are typical of the region: thick, flat udon noodles served in a tamari soy and mackerel-based dashi, noticeably more robust than the bonito-based broths found elsewhere in Japan. Traditional toppings include fish cake, spring onion (scallions) and katsuobushi (dried bonito flakes), though modern versions might feature braised beef, curry or even carbonara-style sauces.

Nagoya also has a strong kissaten culture. These Western-style cafes serve yoshoku – Japanese interpretations of Western dishes – such as ogura toast (thick toast topped with sweet red bean paste and a square of butter), along with classics like tonkatsu and omurice.

AICHI PREFECTURE

Nagoya Station, Aichi・名古屋駅、愛知県

35.1688° N, 136.8824° E

HITSUMABUSHI BENTO

Grilled eel bento・ひつまぶし弁当

This bento features Nagoya's famed dish, hitsumabushi: grilled eel (unagi) served over rice, with dashi broth and a selection of condiments. The name comes from the ohitsu (a wooden lidded tub) in which the meal is traditionally served. The vessel was originally chosen for its durability – unlike ceramic bowls, it wouldn't break during delivery (yes, unagi rice was a delivery meal!). The design of this ekiben's packaging pays homage to that wooden ohitsu. Atsuta Houraiken, the restaurant said to have created hitsumabushi, still operates in Nagoya today.

Hitsumabushi is typically enjoyed in four stages – it's not uncommon to divide the dish into four portions so that you can follow this sequence. First, the eel and rice are eaten as they are, as unadon; second, condiments, such as wasabi, sansho and kizami nori, are added; third, hot dashi is poured over to create a comforting soup (ochazuke). The fourth and final portion is enjoyed however you like. The eel is cut into small pieces and paired with multiple toppings to encourage experimentation, keeping each bite fresh and varied.

Hitsumabushi's enduring popularity comes from the rich, smoky flavour and gentle fattiness of the eel, balanced by bright condiments and the playful, multi-stage way it's eaten – turning one bowl into several distinct experiences.

This ekiben makes special note of using domestic eel, which is said to be raised with greater care and a better diet than imported eel, resulting in improved flavour and texture.

Opening the lid

1. UNAGI (PAGE 132)

Highly prized eel that has been grilled and glazed with kabayaki sauce – a reduction of soy sauce, mirin, sake and sugar. The sauce caramelises as it grills, lending the eel it's characteristic sweet, salty and deeply savoury flavour.

2. MORIGUCHI-ZUKE

A unique pickle to Aichi Prefecture. Moriguchi are a rare variety of radish which grows to over a metre (39 in) long. The daikon is cured for up to three years in mirin and sake lees, producing a sweet, assertive pickle. Seek it out when visiting Aichi.

3. KINSHI TAMAGO (PAGE 27)

Fine strands of lightly sweetened egg.

4. DASHI (PAGE 23)

A light broth of kombu and bonito flakes that moistens the rice and transforms the dish once again.

5. KIZAMI NORI

Finely sliced roasted nori for sprinkling on top of the unagi.

6. SANSHO

A Japanese spice related to Sichuan peppercorn, with citrus notes and gentle numbing heat, traditionally paired with rich foods.

7. WASABI

Fragrant and sharp, wasabi is a perfect condiment for hitsumabushi as it assertively cuts through the fattiness of the eel.

RECIPES ➡

HITSUMABUSHI

Serves 4

GRILLED EEL OVER RICE • ひつまぶし

This recipe uses prepared unagi fillets, which are widely available at Asian grocers (generally labelled as 'unagi kabayaki'). Fresh eel can also be used (see Note). Prepared fillets usually have a stronger sauce flavour as the unagi has already been marinated in the kabayaki sauce, whereas fresh fillets can be grilled to achieve crisp skin and a more smoky flavour.

2 prepared unagi fillets, about 250 g (9 oz) each
400 g (14 oz) steamed rice (page 22), to serve
1 cup kinshi tamago (page 27), approx. 100 g (3½ oz)
2 pinches of sansho pepper powder, to serve
2 tablespoons kizami nori, to serve
2 teaspoons wasabi, to serve

KABAYAKI SAUCE

2 tablespoons sake
2 tablespoons mirin
1 tablespoon zarame or caster (superfine) sugar
2 tablespoons soy sauce

SOUP

500 ml (2 cups) dashi (page 23)
1 tablespoon soy sauce
1 tablespoon sake
1 teaspoon salt

Preheat the oven grill (broiler) to high.

Remove the unagi from the packaging, rinse off the sauce and pat dry. Cut off and reserve the final 5 cm (2 in) of the tail and the first 1 cm (½ in) near the head.

Line a baking tray with foil, grease the foil lightly with neutral oil, and place the unagi fillets on the tray, skin side up. Grill for 10–15 minutes, until the skin is bubbling and lightly browned.

Meanwhile, prepare the kabayaki sauce. In a small saucepan, bring the sake and mirin to the boil and cook for 1 minute, or until reduced by half. Stir in the zarame, soy sauce and the reserved unagi trimmings. Reduce over medium-high heat for 5–10 minutes, until thickened, then remove and discard the eel pieces.

To make the soup, heat the dashi and season with the soy sauce, sake and salt. Keep warm.

Turn the grilled unagi flesh side up, brush generously with the sauce and grill for a further 3–5 minutes, until the sauce is bubbling and glossy. Remove from the heat and brush with more sauce, then slice the eel into 1 cm (½ in) wide strips.

Place the rice in the bento boxes, spoon the remaining sauce over, scatter with the kinshi tamago and top with the unagi. Serve with the hot dashi, sansho pepper, kizami nori and wasabi on the side.

Enjoy first as unadon ('eel on rice'), then with the condiments, and finally add the dashi to finish as ochazuke (comforting soup).

NOTE // USING FRESH EEL FILLETS

Pour boiling water over the eel skin and scrape off any slime. Remove the fins using a knife or scissors. Pierce the skin all over with metal or wooden skewers to prevent bubbling and separation during cooking.

If using a charcoal grill, cook skin side down over high heat for 4–6 minutes, until crisp. Turn and brush the flesh side with the sauce until glazed, then grill for a further 3–5 minutes, until cooked.

Alternatively, preheat the oven grill (broiler) to high and cook the fillets, skin side up, for 3–5 minutes, until crisp. Turn and brush with the sauce, then grill the flesh side for a further 4–5 minutes, until cooked and browned. Slice the unagi and serve as above.

AICHI PREFECTURE

Nagoya Station, Aichi · 名古屋駅、愛知県

35.1688° N, 136.8824° E

MATSUURA NO MISO HIRE KATSU JU

Matsuura's miso tenderloin katsu box · 松浦の味噌ヒレカツ重

Nagoya has a deep affection for dark miso, and its most iconic dish that features this ingredient is miso katsu – a crisp, golden pork cutlet draped in a glossy, mahogany-coloured miso sauce. Despite its appearance, the sauce isn't thick, heavy or cloying; it's surprisingly light, smooth and balanced, enhancing the savoury depth of the pork without overpowering it. The miso flavour leans earthy, with a gentle sweetness.

Japanese mustard provides a sharp, bright counterpoint that cuts through the richness of the pork and miso, while ground sesame adds warmth and a subtle nuttiness. Together, these simple condiments transform a simple pork cutlet into something layered and complex – rich, yet harmonious.

This bento also includes an onsen tamago, a slow-cooked, soft-boiled egg that is rarely found in ekiben. When broken over the katsu, it becomes a second sauce, blending with the miso glaze to create a creamy, luxurious finish. As with Hitsumabushi on page 130, this serving method introduces a new way to enjoy the same dish – a small detail that significantly elevates the eating experience.

This ekiben is produced by Matsuura, a Nagoya-based ekiben maker established in 1922, known for its faithful interpretations of local flavours.

Opening the lid

1. HIRE KATSU (PAGE 136)

Made with pork tenderloin, the cutlet is fried until golden and tender. Even when eaten cold, it remains moist and delicate. The panko crust is soft rather than crunchy, which allows the crumbing to absorb the complex flavour of the miso sauce.

2. MISO DARE (PAGE 137)

'Dare' (or 'tare') just means 'sauce'. Here the defining flavour comes from hatcho miso, a dark, soybean miso that has been aged for 2–3 years and is prized for its deep colour and concentrated umami flavour.

3. ONSEN TAMAGO (PAGE 137)

A gently cooked egg with a barely set white and flowing yolk, traditionally prepared in hot spring water.

4. KARASHI

Sharp, English-style mustard commonly paired with pork dishes, adding heat and palate-cleansing power.

5. SURI GOMA

Optional to add but a welcome flavour when used; ground sesame seeds lend nuttiness and texture to this bento. Sesame is a staple in Nagoya cuisine, appearing famously on tebasaki (Nagoya-style chicken wings).

6. WASABI NO OHITASHI

Dashi-marinated vegetables (page 28) made with wasabi leaf and stem, contributing a fresh, peppery lift.

RECIPES ➡

HIRE KATSU

Serves 4

CRUMBED PORK CUTLET・ヒレカツ

This recipe uses pork tenderloin, though pork loin is another common cut for katsu. If you are using loin, make sure to trim the excess fat before crumbing (page 124). You can substitute pork with chicken or beef if you prefer; ensure the portions are similar in size for even cooking.

- 2 eggs
- 1 tablespoon milk
- 150 g (1 cup) plain (all-purpose) flour
- salt and ground black pepper
- 60 g (1 cup) panko breadcrumbs
- 4 pieces pork tenderloin, about 150 g (5½ oz) each
- neutral oil, for frying

Whisk the eggs and milk in a bowl. Spread the flour on a plate and season with salt and pepper. Place the panko on a separate plate. Line a tray with baking paper.

To crumb the pork, dredge each pork fillet lightly in the flour, shaking off the excess. Dip into the egg mixture, then coat thoroughly with the panko.

Transfer to the lined tray and refrigerate for 5–10 minutes, until ready to fry.

Meanwhile, in a deep, heavy-based frying pan, heat about 2 cm (¾ in) of oil to 160°C (320°F), or until breadcrumbs bubble immediately when added.

Working in batches if necessary, carefully lower the pork into the oil. Fry for about 3 minutes, until golden on one side, then turn and cook for a further 2–3 minutes, until cooked through. Test with a skewer or thermometer to ensure the centre is hot.

Drain on a wire rack and season lightly with salt and pepper.

The pork will keep for up to 1 day in the fridge.

MISO DARE

Serves 4

MISO SAUCE・味噌だれ

This is what sets katsu in Nagoya apart from the katsu in the rest of the country. While other misos are typically a blend of rice and soy beans, hatcho miso is made entirely from soy beans as Nagoya's humidity and heat made rice spoil during the miso fermentation process. Soy beans ferment slower than rice, which is why hatcho miso is aged for at least 2 years (other miso is generally aged for 1–3 months).

- 45 ml (1½ fl oz) dashi (page 23) or water
- 2 tablespoons hatcho miso (about 60 g/2 oz)
- 2 tablespoons caster (superfine) sugar
- 1 tablespoon mirin
- 1 tablespoon oyster sauce

Mix all the ingredients until smooth. Warm gently if serving immediately, then pour over the pork.

ONSEN TAMAGO

Serves 4

ONSEN EGGS・温泉卵

Traditionally made by immersing eggs in the stable, warm waters of an onsen, or hot spring, onsen tamago have become a common addition to many rice bowls. The creamy texture creates an almost risotto-like consistency when mixed into rice. Rice bowls topped with beef or chicken are elevated by the addition of an onsen tamago.

This is a simplified, reliable method for making onsen eggs at home, without any fancy equipment.

- 4 eggs, at room temperature

In a saucepan, bring 1 litre (4 cups) of water to the boil, then turn off the heat. When the bubbling subsides, gently lower the eggs into the water using a slotted spoon.

Leave the eggs in the water for 11 minutes.

Transfer the eggs to a bowl and run under cold water for 1 minute to stop them cooking further.

Refrigerate and use within 48 hours.

NARA

Japan's ancient capital from 710 CE to 794 CE, Nara is a city steeped in history, ritual and preservation. Visitors today come for the roaming deer and to visit the monumental Great Buddha at Todai-ji, but spending time with the region's food offers another way to understand the city's past.

Beyond kakinoha-zushi (persimmon leaf seafood sushi), seek out Miwa somen, a local interpretation of Japan's fine wheat noodles. While somen is usually served cold, in Nara it is often enjoyed hot as nyumen, in a clear broth with spring onion (scallions), fish cake and pork – simple, nourishing, and quietly satisfying.

Desserts are equally memorable. Mochi is everywhere, from street stalls selling kusamochi (page 107) to shops performing traditional mochitsuki (rice pounding). Nakatanidou, near Nara Station, is famous for its lightning-fast demonstrations, drawing crowds daily.

For a deeper taste of culinary history, travel about an hour south of Nara Station to Yasuke Tsurube Sushi, widely considered the oldest sushi restaurant in Japan, with a history extending back more than 800 years. Here, there is no tuna or salmon nigiri. Instead, lightly cured ayu (sweetfish) is grilled and pressed onto rice, reflecting an era before modern refrigeration. Though the original building no longer stands, the current structure, built in 1939, overlooks the stream where the ayu were once caught.

NARA PREFECTURE

Kintetsu-Nara Station, Nara • 近鉄奈良駅、奈良県

34.6850° N, 135.8261° E

TANAKA NO KAKINOHA-ZUSHI

Tanaka's persimmon leaf seafood sushi • たなかの柿の葉すし

From Nara comes one of Japan's most enduring traditional packaged foods: kakinoha-zushi, or persimmon leaf sushi. Lightly cured fish is pressed onto seasoned rice, then wrapped in fragrant persimmon leaves.

Because Nara lies inland from the sea, preserving fish for transport was once essential. Persimmon leaves offered a practical solution. Their natural antibacterial properties help keep the sushi fresh, while also imparting a subtle aroma and gentle sweetness. The result is a style of sushi that is practical, elegant and, most of all, delicious.

Tanaka, the maker of this ekiben, has a history spanning more than 120 years and specialises exclusively in kakinoha-zushi. Their approach is conservative and precise, preserving a taste of the past.

This ekiben contains three classic sushi varieties, each featuring a different species of fish.

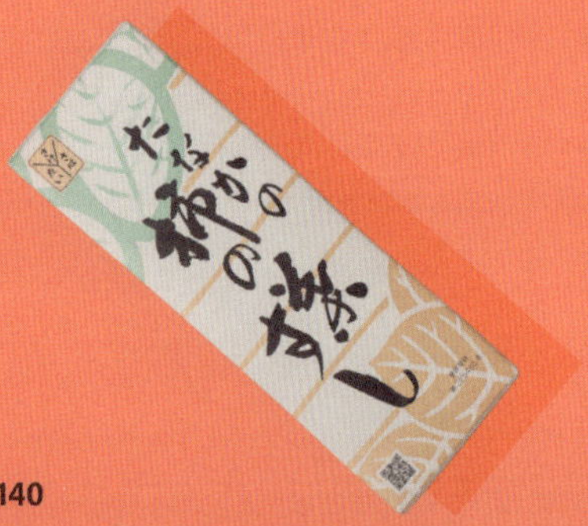

Opening the lid

1. TAI-ZUSHI

Lightly cured sea bream with vinegar and a touch of sugar. The sea bream has a delicate flavour and gently firm texture, its clean taste allows the sweetness of the rice and the faint fragrance of the persimmon leaf to come through clearly.

2. SAKE-ZUSHI

Richer and more full-bodied than sea bream, salmon brings fattiness and depth, providing contrast to the subtlety of the tai.

3. SABA-ZUSHI

Mackerel, traditionally cured with salt and vinegar, has the boldest flavour of the three. The curing tempers any fishiness while adding a pleasant, mouth-watering acidity.

NARA PREFECTURE

Kintetsu-Nara Station, Nara・近鉄奈良駅、奈良県

34.6850° N, 135.8261° E

HANATEMARI

Ball-shaped sushi assortment・花てまり

Temari-zushi, or ball-shaped sushi, are small, decorative sushi made by wrapping toppings over seasoned rice and gently shaping them into spheres. Compared with nigiri or pressed sushi varieties such as kakinoha-zushi (page 140), temari-zushi require little technical skill and are quick to assemble.

The style is said to have originated in Kyoto, where the smaller size made them easier to eat gracefully – an oft-cited reason for their size is that they allowed women to enjoy sushi without smudging their makeup. For this reason, temari-zushi are especially associated with Hinamatsuri, or Girls' Day, celebrated on 3 March. Their bright colours and jewel-like appearance suit festive occasions, seasonal celebrations and gift boxes.

Traditionally shaped using a cloth, temari-zushi can also be formed with plastic wrap. This method of wrapping allows for consistent shapes with minimal trial and error. The result is sushi that is light, elegant and visually striking.

This hanatemari assortment presents a wide range of flavours and textures in miniature form.

Opening the lid

1. NOZAWANA
Sushi rice mixed with sesame seeds and ohitashi nozawana (blanched Japanese turnip greens), lightly seasoned with dashi.

2. SABA
Vinegar-cured mackerel provides a bold, savoury contrast to the rice.

3. SAKE
Salt-cured salmon set over sesame-studded rice, rich yet balanced.

4. EBI
Sweet prawn (shrimp), butterflied and draped over rice, finished with a slice of renkon (lotus root).

5. ANAGO
Rice wrapped in a thin egg sheet and topped with gently simmered anago (saltwater conger eel).

6. TAI
Delicate sea bream accented with slivers of yuzu peel for freshness.

7. TOBIKO GUNKAN
Egg-wrapped sushi filled with flying fish roe and finished with a slice of lemon.

8. MINI CHIRASHI
Sushi rice mixed with aosa (sea lettuce), topped with kinshi tamago (page 27), braised shiitake, boiled prawn (shrimp), edamame and carrot.

RECIPES ➡

TEMARI-ZUSHI

BALL-SHAPED SUSHI・てまり寿司

Makes 20 pieces; serves 2

This basic recipe produces sushi rice suitable for shaping into temari (balls) and topping with fish, egg or vegetables as desired. Please buy your seafood from a reputable supplier.

For a simple variation, boil and butterfly prawns (shrimp), remove the vein, and wrap around rice. Slices of salmon or sea bream provide colour and balance.

Wrapping the rice in a thin egg sheet made from kinshi tamago (page 27) and finishing with salmon roe is another easy and elegant option.

60 ml (¼ cup) rice vinegar
1 tablespoon caster (superfine) sugar
1 teaspoon salt
300 g (10½ oz) cooked sushi rice
20 slices sashimi-grade seafood, such as salmon, sea bream, tuna or prawns (shrimp)

Whisk together the vinegar, sugar and salt until the sugar and salt dissolve. Pour over the warm rice and gently fold in using a spatula, being careful not to crush the grains.

Cover with a damp cloth to keep the rice warm and prevent drying.

Lay a square of plastic wrap or damp cloth on your work surface. Place a slice of seafood, presentation side down, in the centre. Spoon about 15 g (½ oz) – a generous tablespoon – of rice on top.

Gather the corners of the plastic wrap or cloth and twist gently to form a ball. Do not compress too tightly, as this will make the rice dense.

Repeat with the remaining rice and toppings.

The temari-zushi are best enjoyed as soon as possible. Unwrap before eating and serve immediately with soy sauce and gari (sweet pickled ginger).

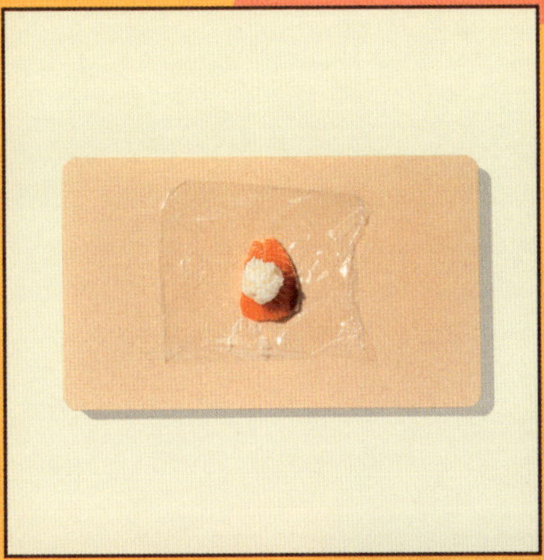

SUPER "DRY"
Asahi
スーパードライ
ピップ
Nov. 25, 2024
Glico
グリコ
雪印メグミルク
牧場の朝
明日も、元気に!
夢ある住まい
エステムシリーズ
日商エステム
かぜに
改源
ZETTERIA
かに道楽
大阪樟蔭女子大学

OSAKA

Osaka is famously described by the phrase kuidaore – 'to eat until you go bankrupt'. In a city where food is abundant, it's an easy fate to meet (even if the food is also very afforable).

Despite its size, Osaka is highly walkable. From Umeda in the north to Namba in the south, the city unfolds as a continuous stretch of eating opportunities: takoyaki stalls, okonomiyaki counters, ramen shops and crab restaurants appear at every turn.

Almost every cuisine is well represented, and meals of comparable quality to Tokyo are often noticeably cheaper, with reservations easier to get. Osaka's food culture is informal, generous and deeply rooted in pleasure – cooking not to impress, but to satisfy. Ekiben in the city reflects this playful nature. You'll find ekiben with takoyaki, kushiyaki (grilled meat on skewers), and even ramen ekiben (Osaka is the home of instant ramen), where rice is topped with chicken, duck and ramen noodles!

OSAKA

Shin-Osaka Station, Osaka · 新大阪駅、大阪府

34.7341° N, 135.5019° E

OSAKA ZUSHI KOKERA RYOSAI

Osaka ryosai sushi box · 大阪寿司こけらりょうさい

During the Meiji period (1868–1912), Yoshino Sushi – a long-established sushi restaurant in Osaka's Senba district, which was founded in 1841 – developed hakozushi, or boxed sushi. This style uses generous amounts of high-quality ingredients such as sea bream, prawns (shrimp) and saltwater conger eel, pressed neatly into compact forms. Easy to transport and visually impressive, hakozushi was ideal as an intermission meal for theatre-goers or as a gift, and quickly became popular among the merchants of Senba. Over time, it spread throughout Osaka and became a standard dish of hospitality.

This ekiben brings together an assortment of hakozushi alongside older, rarely seen styles of sushi, all arranged to fit snugly within a small wooden box. Each piece offers a distinct preparation and flavour, showcasing both the breadth of Osaka's sushi traditions and the maker's skill and restraint.

The name 'kokera' refers to the thin wooden shingles traditionally used for roofing and ryosai means 'vibrant colours' or 'pretty appearance'. The pressed sushi, layered and precise, visually echoes these wooden tiles.

While Osaka's ekiben can be wild, with fried and fatty foods, this distinctly Osaka ekiben shows that the city has always been at the forefront of culinary innovation with a rich history and flavour all its own.

Opening the lid

1. TAI HAKO-ZUSHI

Lightly cured sea bream pressed over rice. Similar in technique to Nara-style sushi (pages 140), but without the persimmon leaf. Clean and restrained.

2. UNAGI HAKO-ZUSHI

Kabayaki-glazed eel arranged on the rice with half the eel skin side up, and half flesh side up, creating a striking contrast. Sweet, smoky and rich, it stands in clear contrast to the delicacy of the tai.

3. MATSUMAE-ZUSHI

An old-style rolled sushi originally made using seaweed from Matsumae, Hokkaido, made famous in Osaka. Salt-and-vinegar-cured mackerel is rolled with rice and topped with a sheet of kombu. Designed for long journeys, both the curing and the kombu's antibacterial properties aid preservation. The soft seaweed intensifies the mackerel's flavour – something to appreciate if you enjoy bold fish character.

4. YAKI-SABA HAKO-ZUSHI

Mackerel marinated in soy sauce and grilled before pressing. The cooking mellows the fishiness, producing a flaky texture and rich, savoury flavour.

5. DATE-MAKI ZUSHI

A distinctly Osaka preparation in which a futomaki (large sushi) roll is wrapped in a thick omelette. The filling includes kanpyo (braised gourd), mushrooms and ebi oboro (crumbled prawn/shrimp).

6. TAI-EBI KOKERA-ZUSHI

Sea bream and prawn (shrimp) combined on a single piece of pressed sushi, offering contrast in texture and sweetness, finished with a kinome leaf.

7. ASEHA ZUSHI-SABA

A large piece of mackerel steamed in aseha leaf. The leaf imparts a fresh, green aroma, while the gently cooked fish remains tender and mild.

8. TAMAGO-EBI KOKERA-ZUSHI

Sweet omelette and prawn (shrimp) share a single piece of hakozushi, a classic pairing where the sweetness of the egg complements the prawn perfectly.

ODA
世界の食材
28000種類
業務用食品スーパー
上海飯店
北京ダック
北京烤鴨店
一口酥香饞遍天下客
挂爐真火美味黄金鴨
中華旬菜 華鳳
http://www.kobe-kaho.com
華鳳名物
本格北京ダッ
本格
北京ダック専門店
炭火直焼き

HYOGO

Hyogo Prefecture stretches from the Sea of Japan to the Seto Inland Sea, a landscape where mountains meet coastlines and history blends with modern life. On the Seto Inland Sea, the coastal city of Akashi, just west of Kobe, is famous for its sweet, tender octopus. Here, ekiben such as Hipparidako celebrate the city's fishing heritage.

The capital, Kobe, is a city of cosmopolitan flair and quiet charm. Its bustling Chinatown hums with the scent of steamed buns and soy, while Showa-era coffee shops, with faded wood and soft jazz, recall a gentler, slower pace of life. Stroll through Motomachi, the longest shopping street in Japan, where boutiques, cafes and markets line the covered arcade, and you'll glimpse the blend of international influence and local tradition that makes Kobe unique.

North of Kobe, Hyogo's farmland is vast. It is Japan's top sake producing region, growing prized Yamada Nishiki rice and brewing it with mineral rich water. There's also Kobe beef, probably the best known Japanese wagyu and one of the most expensive. Here you'll find it regularly in restaurants and it's worth trying. It's densely marbled, meltingly tender, and rich. Just a small amount is enough to sate one's hunger.

HYOGO PREFECTURE

Shin-Kobe Station, Hyogo・新神戸駅、兵庫県

34.7065° N, 135.1956° E

KOBE PORK BUTAMESHI BENTO

Kobe pork meal bento・神戸ポーク豚めし弁当

Kobe may be best known for its beef, but the region's pork is equally impressive, often reaching wagyu-like levels of marbling. This bento features pork from Takao Farm, located just north of Kobe City, where a special breed of black pigs is raised on a diet of corn and bread, alongside pure mineral water pumped from 120 metres (393 feet) underground. The result is pork with even marbling, sweet juicy meat, and soft, clean-tasting fat.

The pork is prepared shoga-yaki style – a comforting, home-style dish of pork cooked with ginger and soy sauce that works equally well for dinner, lunch or bento. Familiar yet deeply satisfying, it's a classic of everyday Japanese cooking.

This bento also features curried potato salad. Kobe is known as a curry city – it was once a main port of Japan, and many Chinese and Indian merchants established themselves there, bringing with them their food culture. Although curry isn't part of Chinese cuisine, the Chinese merchants were connected through trade with South-East Asian countries such as Malaysia, Singapore and Thailand. As a result, many Chinese restaurants in Kobe serve curry and South-East Asian fare. The strong Western culture, as seen in cafes and local architecture, has also strengthened the interest in curry. English-style mild and slightly sweet curry is among the most popular styles of curry in Kobe.

Opening the lid

1. KOBE PORK NO SHOGA-YAKI (PAGE 154)

Thinly sliced pork loin cooked in a fragrant ginger and onion sauce. The pork here is served whole, without trimming the fat; so high is the quality of the pork that the fat is not chewy. Both the meat and fat are tender and flavoursome in the sweet, fragrant sauce.

2. GOHAN (PAGE 22)

Rice cooked in dashi and topped with stewed onions that have absorbed the pork cooking juices, resulting in a gently sweet and savoury base.

3. KARĒ POTETO SARADA (PAGE 155)

A potato salad lightly spiked with curry powder for warmth and depth.

4. KOMATSUNA

Japanese mustard greens cured with rice vinegar, salt, and a touch of chilli for freshness and bite.

RECIPES ➡

SHOGA-YAKI

Serves 2

GINGER PORK STIR-FRY・生姜焼き

A quick, dependable favourite in Japanese home cooking, shoga-yaki is fragrant, comforting and endlessly adaptable. If pork is unavailable, chicken or beef can be substituted; keep the slices around 5 mm (¼ in) to 1 cm (½ in) thick. For a complete home-style meal, serve with finely shredded cabbage and Japanese mayonnaise.

- 300 g (10½ oz) pork loin, sliced about 5 mm (¼ in) thick, or minute steaks (see Note)
- salt and ground black pepper
- 2 tablespoons grated ginger
- 2 tablespoons soy sauce
- 1 tablespoon caster (superfine) sugar
- 1 tablespoon sake
- 1 teaspoon roasted sesame oil
- 2 tablespoons neutral oil
- ½ onion, finely sliced
- 2 tablespoons plain (all-purpose) flour or potato starch
- steamed rice (page 22), to serve

Using the tip of a knife, pierce the pork slices several times all over, focusing on the fat. This step will help tenderise the pork. Season with salt and pepper.

Mix together the ginger, soy sauce, sugar, sake, sesame oil and a couple of pinches of pepper.

Heat the neutral oil in a large frying pan over medium heat. Add the onion and cook for about 3 minutes, until softened and slightly coloured. When ready, push the onion to the side of the pan.

Coat the pork in the flour, shaking off the excess, then sear in the same pan as the onion for 3–4 minutes. When coloured, turn the pork over and pour in the soy mixture. Allow to simmer for 1 minute, or until the pork is cooked.

Spoon the onion over rice, then arrange the pork slices on top. Serve immediately, or allow to cool, then refrigerate and eat the next day.

NOTE //

If you can't find these cuts, use thinly sliced pork belly instead.

KARĒ POTETO SARADA

Serves 4

CURRY POTATO SALAD・カレーポテトサラダ

Potato salad is one of Japan's most popular sides, yet it appears surprisingly rarely in ekiben. This simple curry-flavoured version adds warmth without overwhelming the dish. For a more classic Japanese potato salad, omit the curry powder and add diced boiled egg, ham, pickled carrot and cucumber. Cooked macaroni pasta can also be used in place of potatoes for a macaroni salad.

500 g (1 lb 2 oz) potatoes
1 tablespoon salt
½ teaspoon ground black pepper
2 tablespoons rice vinegar
1 tablespoon dijon mustard
½ teaspoon Japanese curry powder or other mild curry powder
60 g (¼ cup) Japanese mayonnaise

Peel the potatoes and cut into bite-sized chunks.

Place in a large saucepan, cover with cold water and the salt. Bring to the boil, then boil for about 15 minutes, until a skewer or knife goes through easily.

Drain the potatoes and, while still hot, season with a little salt, the pepper, vinegar and mustard. Using a spatula, fold the seasonings through until the potatoes are completely covered. Cool to room temperature.

Mix the curry powder into a paste with 1 teaspoon of boiling water to activate the spices. Add 1 tablespoon of the mayonnaise and mix until incorporated, then mix in the remaining mayonnaise.

When the potatoes have cooled, gently fold the mayonnaise through, then cover and refrigerate until required.

Use within 24 hours.

HYOGO PREFECTURE

Shin-Kobe Station, Hyogo・新神戸駅、兵庫県

34.7065° N, 135.1956° E

KOBE CHUKA SHUMAI BENTO

Kobe Chinese-style pork dumpling bento・神戸中華焼売弁当

Kobe, like Yokohama, is celebrated for its Chinatown, called Nankinmachi, which was established in 1868 when the city's port opened to international trade. Walking its bustling streets, you're met with a riot of sights, sounds and smells: stalls overflowing with filled buns, shumai (steamed pork dumplings), skewers, noodles and Peking duck, while restaurants spill onto the sidewalks with plastic food displays and brightly lettered menus. Tourists and locals alike jostle for shengjian bao – crispy-bottomed, soup-filled dumplings – or guabao, soft buns stuffed with braised pork belly. The sheer variety is thrilling, though quality can be uneven; a long queue is usually a good sign, while empty shops are often best avoided.

Kobe's ekiben, such as the Kobe Chuka Shumai Bento, bring the flavours of Nankinmachi to the train platform, combining savoury steamed dumplings with a selection of small, boldly flavoured Chinese-inspired dishes.

Opening the lid

1. SHUMAI

Steamed pork dumplings that are soft and juicy, carrying the delicate fragrance of ginger and sesame. These are slightly softer and more onion-forward than the Yokohama-style shumai on page 112.

2. EBI CHILLI (PAGE 158)

Tender prawns (shrimp), deep-fried and coated in a mildly spicy, sweet chilli sauce, providing a lively contrast to the dumplings.

3. MAPO TOFU (PAGE 159)

Firm tofu in a rich, savoury, gently spicy sauce. This is a very mild version of mapo tofu, suitable even for those who avoid heat.

4. TAKANA

Chinese-style pickled mustard greens with a tangy, fermented flavour that pairs well with pork shumai.

5. BIHUN

Vermicelli noodles cooked in a chicken-flavoured broth. The noodles have a chewy texture and mild flavour.

6. TAWARA GATA GOHAN

Rice shaped into small cylinders that have been sprinkled with sesame seeds. The shape makes it easy to pick up while travelling, while the seeds add a pleasant crunch.

RECIPES ➡

EBI CHILLI

Serves 4 as part of a shared meal

DEEP-FRIED CHILLI PRAWNS・エビチリ

In Japan, chilli often signals flavour and sweetness rather than heat, and this dish is a perfect example. The prawns are lightly battered and fried, then coated in a fragrant, sweet, gently spicy sauce. The crisp coating absorbs the sauce, giving each bite a satisfying balance of the bouncy prawn and the savoury sweetness of doubanjiang and ketchup, with just a hint of chilli warmth.

1½ tablespoons salt
1½ tablespoons caster (superfine) sugar
300 g (10½ oz) prawns (shrimp), peeled and deveined
1 litre (4 cups) neutral oil, for deep-frying
50 g (1¾ oz) potato starch
1 egg
50 g (⅓ cup) plain (all-purpose) flour
1 teaspoon rice vinegar
1 teaspoon chilli oil (optional)

SAUCE

2 tablespoons neutral oil
2 garlic cloves, minced
1 cm (½ in) piece ginger, peeled and minced
2 teaspoons doubanjiang (spicy chilli bean paste)
3 spring onions (scallions), finely sliced, white and green parts separated
1 teaspoon caster (superfine) sugar
½ teaspoon salt
½ teaspoon chicken stock powder
2 tablespoons tomato ketchup
1 tablespoon potato starch

Mix the salt and sugar in a bowl with 500 ml (2 cups) water until the salt and sugar dissolve. Add the prawns, mix well and allow to cure for 30 minutes.

Meanwhile, prepare the sauce. Heat the neutral oil over medium heat, then add the garlic, ginger and doubanjiang. Turn the heat down to medium–low and fry for about 2 minutes, until the oil turns red. Add the spring onion whites, mix briefly, then add the sugar, salt and stock powder, followed by 250 ml (1 cup) water. Bring to the boil, then stir the ketchup through.

Mix the potato starch with 2 tablespoons water and add half to the boiling sauce, stirring to disperse and thicken. Bring back to the boil. If the sauce is not thick enough, stir in the remaining potato starch liquid, otherwise discard it. Set aside.

In a deep, heavy-based pan, heat the deep-frying oil to 160°C (320°F).

Drain the prawns and dry thoroughly.

Place the potato starch on a tray. In a bowl, combine the egg with the flour, then add the prawns and massage in thoroughly.

Working one at a time, coat the prawns in the potato starch, then deep-fry for 2 minutes, in batches if needed to avoid overcrowding the pan.

Remove to a wire rack to drain.

Increase the oil temperature to 180°C (350°F). Refry the prawns for about 2 minutes, until golden and crisp.

Drain the prawns on the wire rack, then add to the sauce and mix through and heat lightly over medium heat. Leave to simmer for 1 minute, then stir in the vinegar, and chilli oil, if using. Taste and adjust with salt, sugar or vinegar as needed.

Serve immediately, or allow to cool, then refrigerate and use within 2 days.

MAPO TOFU

麻婆豆腐

Serves 4 as part of a shared meal

This mapo tofu is less saucy than versions you might be used to, reflecting the practical needs of ekiben, which must travel and be eaten without spilling. What sauce remains is packed with flavour from the doubanjiang bean paste and Sichuan pepper.

Rather than being eaten with rice, as is traditional, this version uses firm tofu cut into large cubes, making it easy to pick up with chopsticks, and eaten on its own.

300 g (10½ oz) firm tofu, ideally momen ('cloth-pressed') tofu
1 teaspoon sesame oil
1 teaspoon neutral oil
100 g (3½ oz) minced (ground) pork
1 leek, white part only, diced
1 garlic clove, minced
1 teaspoon minced ginger
1 tablespoon aka miso (red miso paste)
1 tablespoon doubanjiang (spicy chilli bean paste)
1 tablespoon caster (superfine) sugar
3 tablespoons sake
2 tablespoons soy sauce
1 tablespoon oyster sauce
1 teaspoon chicken stock powder
200 ml (7 fl oz) water or chicken stock
1½ tablespoons cornflour (corn starch), mixed with 3 tablespoons water
½ teaspoon ground Sichuan peppercorns

Bring a saucepan of water to the boil.

Cut the tofu into 1.5 cm (½ in) cubes and blanch in the boiling water for 1 minute. Remove and allow to drain, discarding the water.

In a frying pan, heat the sesame oil and neutral oil over medium-low heat. Fry the pork for about 5 minutes, breaking it into smaller pieces, cooking the pork until cooked through and the liquid has evaporated.

Stir in the leek, garlic and ginger and cook for 3–5 minutes, until softened.

Add the miso paste, doubanjiang and sugar, stirring until fragrant.

Stir in the sake, soy sauce, oyster sauce, stock powder, and water or chicken stock.

Finally, add the tofu and bring back to the boil. While gently stirring, add the cornflour slurry and cook, stirring, for about 1 minute, until the sauce has thickened. Finish with the Sichuan pepper.

Serve immediately, or allow to cool, then refrigerate and use within 3 days.

HYOGO PREFECTURE

Akashi Station, Hyogo · 明石駅、兵庫県

34.6491° N, 134.9927° E

AKASHI MEIBUTSU HIPPARIDAKO MESHI

Akashi's famous Hipparidako meal · 明石名物ひっぱりだこ飯

Hipparidako, literally 'pulled octopus,' is an expression meaning to be 'in high demand'. It comes from the way octopus is dried, with its arms spread out in all directions, that resembles it being pulled by many people. The ekiben has cleverly used the name to reference the contents and as marketing. This ekiben lives up to the name though, as it has become extremely popular.

The bento is served in a ceramic vessel inspired by a tako-tsubo, the traditional clay pot used to catch octopus. Once the meal is finished, the pot can be reused for storage or as a cup. In the city of Akashi, where this ekiben originates from, you'll find the vessels with handles already attached as a mug to take home as a souvenir!

Hipparidako meshi celebrates Akashi's long history of octopus fishing, showcasing tender braised octopus alongside a variety of carefully prepared seasonal components, one of them artfully hidden beneath the rice.

Opening the lid

1. TAKO NO NIMONO (PAGE 162)

Two pieces of octopus braised gently in dashi. The texture remains lightly chewy, releasing the subtle flavour of the dashi with each bite.

2. NANOHANA NO SHOYUZUKE (PAGE 164)

Nanohana (rapeseed greens, similar to cime di rapa/broccoli rabe), cured in soy sauce and citrus. This spring vegetable has a mild bitterness and floral freshness.

3. ANAGO

Finely diced braised saltwater conger eel scattered through the rice, adding bursts of savoury sweetness.

4. YASAI NO TOSA-NI (PAGE 163)

Bamboo shoot, shiitake mushrooms and carrot braised in dashi and finished with bonito flakes. The vegetables are full of umami, with the bamboo shoot retaining a pleasant crunch.

5. TAKIKOMI GOHAN (PAGE 162)

Local rice cooked in the octopus braising liquid, lightly perfumed with the sea and carrying a faint, appealing bitterness.

6. KINSHI TAMAGO (PAGE 27)

Fine strands of softly fried egg for colour and gentle sweetness.

7. TAKO KAMABOKO (PAGE 163)

Hidden at the bottom of the pot is a final surprise: an octopus fish cake, offering one last bite of octopus to end the meal.

RECIPES ➡

TAKO NO NIMONO

Serves 4

BRAISED OCTOPUS・たこの煮物

Braised octopus is a prized dish in Japan. Local Hyogo octopus is large, fresh and retains a pleasing chew even after cooking. Its ability to absorb flavour makes it ideal for gentle braising. Here, the rice is simmered in the broth the octopus is braised in.

This recipe makes enough octopus to eat some on its own, and some to use in the tako kamaboko (octopus fish cake balls).

- 500 g (1 lb 2 oz) fresh octopus tentacles
- 1 tablespoon baking soda
- 2 tablespoons caster (superfine) sugar
- 3 cm (1¼ in) piece kombu
- 2 tablespoons soy sauce
- 1 teaspoon salt
- 300 g (10½ oz) short-grain white rice
- kinshi tamago (page 27), to serve

Sprinkle the octopus with the baking soda and massage for about 5 minutes, until the meat relaxes and becomes tender.

Rinse off the baking soda.

Bring 1 litre (4 cups) water to the boil in a saucepan. Add the octopus, sugar and kombu.

Reduce the heat to low and simmer for 10 minutes.

Add the soy sauce and salt and simmer for a further 10 minutes.

Test the octopus with a skewer; the octopus is ready if the skewer goes through easily. If not, continue cooking for a further 10 minutes.

Remove from the heat and allow the octopus to cool, either in the broth, by transferring the octopus and the cooking liquid to a bowl that is held over ice, or cool the octopus and cooking liquid on the kitchen bench.

Strain the liquid from the octopus through muslin cloth, reserving the braising liquid and octopus separately. Cut the octopus into bite-sized pieces, reserving two tentacles for the tako kamaboko (opposite).

Taste the braising liquid and add salt and sugar to taste – sometimes the octopus is quite salty, other times less so.

Wash the rice until the water runs clear.

Add the washed rice to a donabe, lidded saucepan or rice cooker along with about 350 ml (12 fl oz) of the cooled octopus braising liquid (or enough liquid to reach the level recommended by the rice cooker manufacturer, top up with water or dashi as needed). Follow the instructions on page 22 to soak and cook the rice.

To assemble the ekiben, place a tako kamaboko in the bottom, top with rice, then kinshi tamago, followed by vegetables and octopus.

Once assembled, it will keep in the fridge for up to 2 days.

TAKO KAMABOKO

Makes 12

OCTOPUS FISH CAKE BALLS・たこかまぼこ

- 2 braised octopus tentacles, from the tako no nimono (opposite)
- 60 g (2 oz) hanpen (white fish paste)
- 40 g (1½ oz) prawn (shrimp) meat, deveined
- 1 egg
- 1 tablespoon Japanese mayonnaise
- neutral oil, for deep-frying

Cut the skin and suckers from the octopus tentacles. Slice off 12 small pieces, about 1 cm (½ in) long. Weigh 40 g (1½ oz) of the remaining octopus tentacles and roughly chop.

In a food processor, blend the hanpen, prawn meat, egg and mayonnaise until smooth.

Add the chopped octopus and process again until only small pieces of octopus remain. Make 12 balls with the mix, adding a piece of octopus to the centre of each.

In a deep heavy-based saucepan, heat about 5 cm (2 in) of oil to 180°C (350°F).

Deep-fry the octopus cakes in batches for 5–6 minutes, turning halfway through. They're done when a skewer inserted in the middle comes out clean.

Carefully remove from the oil, then drain on paper towel.

Serve straight away, or allow to cool, then refrigerate for up to 3 days.

YASAI NO TOSA-NI

Serves 4

VEGETABLES IN TOSA-STYLE BRAISE・野菜の土佐煮

Tosa-ni means 'in the style of Tosa', a seaside town on Shikoku Island. This cooking method involves braising ingredients in dashi and sprinkling them with bonito flakes to finish. Tosa is known for katsuo or bonito (skipjack tuna) fishing and was the origin of both katsuobushi – fermented, smoked shaved bonito flakes, so integral to modern Japanese cooking – and katsuo no tataki (seared bonito sashimi), which is served in izakayas across the country.

- 4 dried shiitake mushrooms
- 1 whole cooked bamboo shoot (tinned or vacuum-packed), about 100 g (3½ oz)
- 500 ml (2 cups) dashi (page 23)
- 1 tablespoon caster (superfine) sugar
- 2 tablespoons mirin
- 2 tablespoons soy sauce
- 2 tablespoons sake
- 1 tablespoon katsuobushi (bonito flakes)

Soak the shiitake in hot water for 15 minutes.

Cut the bamboo shoots into thin wedges and place in a saucepan with the dashi. Bring up to a gentle boil, then simmer over medium heat for 15 minutes.

Drain the shiitake and add to the pan, along with the sugar, mirin, soy sauce and sake. Cover with a cartouche (a round of baking paper with a small hole cut in the centre) and simmer for a further 15 minutes.

When the liquid has reduced, turn off the heat. Sprinkle the bonito flakes over, stir gently, and allow to cool. Transfer to a container and refrigerate overnight before using.

The dish will keep in the fridge for up to 3 days.

NANOHANA NO SHOYUZUKE

Serves 4

SOY PICKLED RAPESEED GREENS・菜の花の醤油漬け

Unlike many Japanese pickles, this preparation is not defined by sharp acidity. Preservation comes primarily from salt and soy sauce, giving the nanohana a pronounced savoury salinity rather than sourness. That intensity is gently balanced with citrus and kombu, which soften the edges and add depth.

Small additions can easily change the character of the dish: a pinch of dried chilli introduces gentle heat, while mustard adds sharpness.

3 cm (1¼ in) piece kombu
juice of ½ yuzu or lemon
125 ml (½ cup) soy sauce
1 tablespoon sake
1 tablespoon mirin
1 bunch nanohana (rapeseed greens) or cime di rapa or broccoli rabe

Using scissors, cut the kombu into thin strips. Place in a small bowl with the yuzu juice, soy sauce, sake and mirin and mix together.

Bring a saucepan of water to the boil. Prepare a bowl of iced cold water.

Cut off the bottom of the nanohana and rinse with plenty of water to remove the dirt.

Blanch in the boiling water for 20–30 seconds, drain, then place in the cold water.

Once cooled, remove from the water and squeeze thoroughly to remove the excess liquid.

Place the boiled greens in a container and pour the soy mixture over. Place a weight (such as another container) on top to press down and submerge the greens.

Marinate in the fridge at least overnight, or up to 3 days.

Lightly squeeze out the liquid, then cut into bite-sized pieces to serve.

HIMEJI

Although not a prefecture, Himeji deserves a special mention, as it feels markedly different from nearby Kobe. For most visitors, the city's focal point is Himeji Castle, one of Japan's best-preserved castles, completed in 1609 and surrounded by expansive parkland. Its brilliant white exterior is unlike any other in the country, earning it the nickname Shirasagi-jo, the White Heron Castle.

While in Himeji, seek out local specialties such as Himeji oden, a comforting one-pot stew distinguished by its warming ginger note layered onto familiar oden flavours. Another must-try is akashiyaki, from the nearby city of Akashi. A softer, egg-rich cousin to takoyaki (octopus dumpling balls), and served dipped in hot dashi, akashiyaki are inexpensive, comforting and satisfying, especially on colder days.

__HIMEJI CITY, HYOGO PREFECTURE__

Himeji Station, Hyogo・姫路駅、兵庫県

34.8264° N, 134.6908° E

HIMEJI JO GO-SO ANAGO MESHI

Five-tier sea eel rice・姫路城五層あなごめし

Modelled after the five tiers of Himeji Castle, this ekiben highlights one of the region's most beloved specialties: anago, or sea eel (also called saltwater conger eel). Unlike unagi (freshwater eel), which is typically grilled over charcoal, anago is gently braised in soy sauce, sake and mirin until the flesh becomes soft and the fine bones are tender enough to eat. The flavour is less rich than unagi, with the skin contributing a light gelatinousness that gives the fish a subtle, luxurious texture. Some diners prefer the smoky intensity of grilled unagi; others favour the soft, 'fluffy' character of braised anago.

In this ekiben, the anago is lightly grilled after braising, adding a faint wisp of smoke to its natural sweetness. The anago is then layered over rice, alternating with thick pieces of tamago. The result is an elegant ekiben that respectfully showcases Himeji's charms.

Opening the lid

1. ANAGO

Sea eel simmered in soy, sake and mirin until tender, then lightly grilled. The flesh flakes delicately, while the skin provides gentle richness without heaviness.

2. DASHIMAKI TAMAGO (PAGE 26)

A sweet-savoury omelette cut to mirror the size of the anago, adding colour and matching the eel's fluffy texture.

3. GOHAN

Rice lightly flavoured with the anago braising liquid, carrying subtle sweetness and umami.

SANSHO AND KABAYAKI SAUCE

Small packets of Japanese pepper and sweet reduced soy sauce are included, allowing you to season each bite to taste.

TOWARDS THE SETTING SUN

Leaving the Kansai plain, the train threads between sea and mountains. The land narrows, then opens again. In Okayama and Hiroshima, fertile plains meet sheltered waters, and cooking reflects this balance – rice grown in abundance, seafood drawn from calm inland seas, flavours rounded rather than sharp. Preservation is less of a concern here; fish is grilled simply, vegetables simmered gently.

In places like Tottori, ingredients are dictated by what survives wind and sand, mountains and coast pressed tightly together. Bento speak of austerity and focus rather than abundance, a quiet reflection of the land itself.

Then the island of Kyushu announces itself. The climate shifts, citrus appears, sweetness and richness move forward. In the port cities of Fukuoka and Nagasaki, food carries echoes of trade and adaptation – sugar, soy, wheat, techniques absorbed and reinterpreted over centuries. Ekiben reflects a region comfortable with change and experimentation. Here, free-spiritedness and resilience coexist, shaped by trade, weather and history.

As the journey approaches its southern edge, from Miyazaki onwards, the pace eases further. Fields glow under wide skies, and meals feel unhurried, generous, grounded rather than showy. Cooking here is shaped by warmth and sun, by long growing seasons and a closeness to both land and sea that feels immediate, tactile, alive.

By the final stations, the sense of endurance that marked the opening chapters of our journey has softened. The logic remains the same: food shaped by land, climate and patience. From snow-dark seas to sunlit fields, the journey closes not with contrast but with continuity – a long, quiet conversation between place and appetite, carried from north to west until the day finally comes to rest.

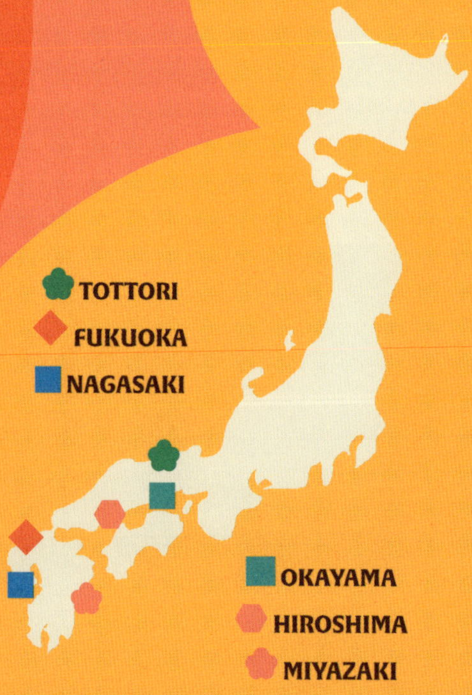

OKAYAMA

Okayama is considered the heart of Japanese denim. The city of Kurashiki, and particularly the district of Kojima, is the birthplace of Japanese indigo-dyed denim. What began as a collection of small family workshops grew into a global reputation built on obsessive attention to dyeing, weaving and finishing, and on a shared belief that denim should improve with time and wear. Visiting Okayama to buy jeans is considered a pilgrimage – so-called 'denim heads' come to acknowledge this fabric that carries the marks of patience, labour and place.

That same sense of considered craft runs through the food. Bara-chirashi, the foundation of matsuri-zushi, anchors local gatherings. Vinegared rice is scattered with seafood from the Seto Inland Sea – prawns (shrimp), anago (saltwater conger eel), mackerel. The dish is colourful and celebratory, and is meant to be shared.

The prefecture is known for its peaches, and peach-based sweets such as pies and jellies abound, but beyond that, Okayama is famed for its large, translucent Shine Muscat grapes, grown to exacting standards. Perfect bunches are displayed in department stores like jewellery, each grape unblemished, impossibly sweet and bursting with juice.

Rising above all this is Okayama Castle, its black exterior once earning it the name 'Crow Castle'. Nearby, Korakuen Garden offers one of Japan's most refined strolling landscapes, designed to be appreciated slowly, step by step. Together, they frame the prefecture's character: deliberate, balanced, and confident enough to let quality speak for itself – whether in cloth, cuisine or craft.

OKAYAMA PREFECTURE

Okayama Station, Okayama・岡山駅、岡山県

34.6668° N, 133.9183° E

MOMOTARO NO MATSURI-ZUSHI

Momotaro festival sushi・桃太郎の祭ずし

The Peach Boy, Momotaro, is everywhere in Okayama – drawn from a foundational local folktale that tells a story of courage, friendship and justice, centred on a boy discovered inside a giant peach floating down a river. The tale is widely known throughout Japan and has inspired countless retellings across film, anime and video games. Momotaro was even the subject of Japan's first feature-length animated film, *Momotaro: Sacred Sailors* (1945), though this was a wartime propaganda piece that portrayed Momotaro and his animal companions as officers in the Japanese army.

This ekiben returns the character to his folkloric roots. The label depicts Momotaro setting out to defeat demons plaguing his hometown, while the rounded box references the peach from which he was born.

Matsuri-zushi is an Okayama specialty: a celebratory form of chirashi-zushi ('scattered sushi'), made without ingredients such as dried gourd or lotus root, which are typically mixed into the rice. This version was specifically developed for long-distance travel and was first produced for the journey between Okayama and Tokyo in 1964, the year of the Tokyo Olympics. Before the Shinkansen connected the country, the trip took more than nine hours. With summer heat and no refrigeration, ekiben had to be carefully designed to last. Every element of this bento reflects that requirement, relying on curing, pickling and thorough cooking to ensure it remains delicious hours into the journey.

Opening the lid

1. SU-MESHI

Lightly vinegared sushi rice made with Okayama-grown Asahi rice. The grains are large with a faintly fruity aroma, qualities that also make the rice well suited to sake brewing. A layer of kinshi tamago (page 27) forms a bright canvas for the toppings above it. Despite its plain appearance, the rice is surprisingly addictive on its own, turning this dish into a celebration of local grain.

2. EBI

A small whole prawn (shrimp) marinated in dashi, sweet and lightly crunchy. It can be eaten whole if desired.

3. SAWARA

A thick slice of pickled Spanish mackerel with a clean, satisfying flavour. A staple of Okayama cuisine, it takes pride of place near the centre of the box.

4. ANAGO

Grilled sea eel brings gentle smokiness from the grill and sweetness from its glaze.

5. SABA

Thin, butterflied, vinegar-cured mackerel with a pleasant acidity and glossy finish.

6. MOGAI-NI

Small cockles lightly simmered in soy sauce, chewy with a faint beach-like aroma.

7. TAKO

Boiled and lightly pickled octopus completes the generous array of seafood, each prepared differently to create contrast in flavour and texture. All are cooked, cured or pickled to ensure the bento tastes as good hours later as it did when first packed.

8. SEISAIZUKE, RENKON, SHIITAKE AND TAKENOKO

Japanese mustard greens, lotus root, shiitake mushrooms and bamboo shoots round out the box, adding colour, crunch and balance.

HIROSHIMA

Hiroshima Prefecture is inseparable from its history, yet it is not defined by solemnity alone. Everyday life here is warm, social and outward-looking. At its centre is Hiroshima-style okonomiyaki. Built in layers rather than being mixed all together, it stacks cabbage, noodles, pork, egg and batter into a carefully constructed savoury pancake that is cooked on a hotplate before you. It is filling and fun – the kind of dish made for late nights and conversation.

The Seto Inland Sea shapes much of the rest of the local cuisine. Hiroshima's oysters are among the most celebrated in Japan, grown in calm, nutrient-rich waters that give them depth of flavour and sweetness. They appear everywhere: raw, grilled, fried or folded into rice. Another local staple is anago (saltwater conger eel), often served alongside oysters. Anago don (sweet, delicate eel over rice), paired with crisp kaki-fry (panko-crumbed, deep-fried oysters) is a combination hard to beat anywhere in the country.

Offshore lies Miyajima, with the floating torii of Itsukushima Shrine. At high tide, the gate appears to hover above the water, serene and unmistakable. Eating here – grilled oysters, still-warm momiji manju maple-leaf cakes – feels inseparable from place. Just beware the deer, who will eat anything unguarded.

HIROSHIMA PREFECTURE

Hiroshima Station, Hiroshima · 広島駅、広島県

34.3978° N, 132.4756° E

RYORI BENTO AJIROYA CHUBO

Ajiroya Kitchen's Cuisine bento · 料理弁当あじろや厨房

This is an example of a two-tier ekiben. Historically, bento with multiple layers were priced higher and considered more premium than single-tier boxes. While that distinction has softened in recent years, with ekiben makers now choosing layered boxes more on design rather than the status of ingredients, this remains an unmistakably luxurious bento, featuring a wide range of local ingredients that have been carefully prepared.

Ajiroya, established in 1901, was Hiroshima's first ekiben producer. Hiroshima's food culture is notably diverse, but two ingredients stand out above all others: oysters and anago (saltwater conger eel). Many local restaurants serve them together as a set, something I highly recommend sampling when visiting.

This bento, however, centres on moburi, a regional style of bara-zushi in which ingredients are mixed directly into the rice. ('Moburi' is Hiroshima dialect for 'to mix' or 'to blend'.) Unlike many forms of sushi familiar to travellers, moburi uses cooked seafood and vegetables, rather than raw ones, making it especially well suited to bento. It originated as a simple, nourishing meal for people working in the fields and was sometimes shaped into musubi (ball shapes) for ease of carrying.

Ajiroya also produces an alternative version of this bento, replacing the moburi layer with anago gohan, featuring thick slices of braised conger eel over rice.

Opening the lid

1. MOBURI (PAGE 182)
The signature element of this ekiben. While moburi can include beans, diced eel or other seafood, this version is intentionally restrained: kinshi tamago (finely shredded soft omelette, page 27), soy-marinated salmon roe, braised lotus root, shiitake mushrooms and green peas. Light in flavour but satisfying, it pairs well with the richer items in the box.

2. TORINIKU NO NARUTO MAKI (PAGE 186)
Tempura-fried chicken rolled with umeboshi (pickled plum) and shiso leaves. Though the batter softens with long sitting, the batter and the rolling technique keep the chicken moist, while the shiso and plum add brightness and acidity.

3. MATSUKAZE-YAKI (PAGE 185)
Minced chicken is seasoned with miso and baked, then cooled and cut into bite-sized blocks. Soft and savoury, it's finished with a scattering of white poppy seeds. Matsukaze-yaki is a classic Osechi ryori (traditional Japanese New Year dish). Dishes for Japanese New Year are prepared ahead to be eaten for the first three days of the new year, allowing for a period of rest, as using knives or cooking is considered bad luck during this time.

4. KOYA TOFU
Freeze-dried tofu, often associated with shojin ryori (temple cuisine). This tofu has been rehydrated and simmered in seasoned dashi, it absorbs flavour readily, developing a chewy, sponge-like texture that is far more enjoyable than it sounds.

5. TAMANEGI NO MARINE
Lightly pickled onion, gently pungent yet refreshing, that has been topped with a single goji berry.

6. YAKI-KAMO (PAGE 183)
A slice of skewered duck breast, cooked medium, adding richness and depth to the ekiben.

7. SATO-IMO (PAGE 184)
Soft-simmered taro, cut into a lantern shape and topped with kinome miso. Sweetness from miso and spiciness from the kinome pair with the taro.

8. DASHIMAKI TAMAGO (PAGE 26)
A generous slice of soft, rolled omelette.

9. SATSUMA-AGE TO FU
Simmered vegetables accompanied with fried fish cake and fu (wheat gluten) which have been rehydrated in dashi until tender.

RECIPES ➡

MOBURI

Serves 4

HIROSHIMA MIXED SUSHI・もぶり

Once a humble worker's meal, moburi has become a celebratory dish for festivals and gatherings. The toppings are traditionally an odd number, considered auspicious, and the rice may be shaped into balls (musubi) and shared as a kind of edible good luck charm.

Additional vegetables can be mixed in, similar to takikomi gohan (rice cooked in seasoned broth), with carrot and burdock root common additions. In Otake, a small city southwest of Hiroshima, black beans (kuromame) are considered essential.

- 300 g (10½ oz) short-grain white rice
- 1 teaspoon salt
- 4 dried shiitake mushrooms
- 100 g (3½ oz) lotus root
- 250 ml (1 cup) dashi (page 23)
- 2 tablespoons soy sauce
- 1½ tablespoons caster (superfine) sugar
- 1 tablespoon sake
- 40 g (¼ cup) fresh or frozen peas
- ¼ cup kinshi tamago (page 27), approx. 25 g (1 oz)
- 2 tablespoons ikura (page 64)

Wash the rice until the water runs clear.

Place the washed rice in a donabe, lidded saucepan or rice cooker along with the salt and 250–375 ml (1–1½ cups) water (or enough liquid to reach the level recommended by the rice cooker manufacturer). Follow the instructions on page 22 to soak and cook the rice.

Meanwhile, place the dried shiitake in a heatproof bowl, cover with hot water and leave to rehydrate for 15 minutes. Discard the soaking liquid, then squeeze the excess liquid from the shiitake.

Peel the lotus root, cut into quarters lengthways, then into 5 mm (¼ in) thick slices. Keep them submerged in water to prevent discolouration.

In a saucepan, bring the dashi, soy sauce, sugar and sake to the boil. Add the shiitake and lotus root and simmer for 15 minutes. Add the peas and cook for a further 3 minutes.

Drain the vegetables, discarding the liquid. Allow to cool, then slice the shiitake thinly.

Mix the vegetables into the cooked rice. Serve topped with the kinshi tamago and ikura.

The moburi can be prepared a day ahead and refrigerated.

YAKI-KAMO

Serves 1 as a main or 4 in an ekiben

GRILLED DUCK WITH SANSHO・焼き鴨

Yaki-kamo is a versatile duck preparation that can be served in bento, soups or as a main course with various side dishes such as the Sato-imo to kinome-miso (taro with kinome miso) or Nimono (braised vegetables, page 29).

The key to getting crispy duck skin is to rest the duck uncovered in the fridge, ideally for 24 hours, to dry the skin thoroughly. When cooking, make sure to slowly render the fat out of the duck breast. Keeping the temperature low is the secret to achieving crisp skin.

1 duck breast
1 teaspoon salt
½ teaspoon sansho pepper powder

Using a sharp knife, remove any silver skin from the underside of the duck breast. Rub the salt over the skin and meat, then rub the sansho pepper over only the flesh. (Only season the meat side with the sansho, as the skin side of the duck breast is pan-fried for a much longer time, which would cause the sansho to burn.)

Place the duck, skin side up, on a rack with a tray underneath. Leave uncovered in the fridge for up to 24 hours, but at least 2 hours.

When ready to cook, use a sharp knife to cut incisions down the duck skin, along the length of the breast, about 2 mm (1⁄16 inch) deep and 1 cm (½ inch) apart. This creates channels for the duck fat to render out, resulting in a crispier skin.

Place the duck, skin side down, in a cold frying pan and turn the heat to medium–low. Cook for 15 minutes without turning the duck breast; there should be a light frying noise. Every 5 minutes, drain the fat from the pan, reserving it for roasted potatoes or stir-fries.

After 15 minutes, turn the duck over onto the flesh side and sear all the parts that appear uncooked, which should only take about a minute.

After you've seared each side, turn the duck on the flesh side for a further minute, then transfer to a plate and allow to rest for 5 minutes.

Slice the duck, then skewer if desired.

The duck can be prepared a day ahead and refrigerated.

SATO-IMO TO KINOME MISO MAKI

Serves 4

TARO WITH KINOME MISO・里芋と木の芽味噌

Sato-imo, or taro, is a starchy, comforting addition to bento. In this dish, the taro is simmered in dashi until tender, then topped with flavoured miso. Here, kinome – the young leaf of the Japanese pepper tree – perfumes the miso with a fresh, citrusy aroma. If you are not able to source kinome, use celery leaf.

For an even simpler miso topping, a little yuzu juice and zest works well, or simply use plain miso, which is still delicious.

- 500 g (1 lb 2 oz) taro, roughly tennis-ball sized if possible (about 4–6 smaller taro)
- 1 litre (4 cups) dashi (page 23)
- 2 tablespoons mirin
- 2 tablespoons soy sauce

KINOME MISO

- 1 handful kinome leaves or celery leaves
- 1 tablespoon sake
- 1 tablespoon mirin
- 1 tablespoon caster (superfine) sugar
- 80 g (2¾ oz) shiro miso (white miso paste)
- ¼ teaspoon sansho pepper powder (optional)

To make the kinome miso, grind the kinome or celery leaves into a fine paste, using a food processor or mortar and pestle.

Warm the sake and mirin in a small saucepan. Add the sugar and stir until dissolved. Remove from the heat and mix in the miso, then fold in the leaf paste and sansho, if using. Refrigerate until needed.

Peel the taro and wash under cold running water to remove any dirt. Cut into pieces the size of ping-pong balls and place in a saucepan, then cover with cold water. Bring to the boil, reduce to a simmer, then cook for 5–8 minutes, until a skewer passes through with slight resistance. Drain.

Transfer the taro to a clean saucepan. Pour in the dashi, mirin and soy sauce and bring to a gentle simmer. Cook for a further 10 minutes, then remove from the heat and allow to cool in the liquid. Refrigerate in the liquid until required; the taro will keep for up to 5 days.

To serve, remove the taro from the broth and coat with the kinome miso for bento. Alternatively, reheat gently in the liquid, plate with a little of the cooking broth, and spoon the kinome miso over the top.

MATSUKAZE-YAKI

Makes 9–16 pieces

松風焼き

This is a long-lasting chicken loaf that freezes well and adds variety and a good source of protein to bento.

The name of the dish is quite interesting. It's too complicated to go into here, but it refers to a Noh (a classical Japanese musical drama) play about a ghost named Matsukaze who longs for her lover.

1 dried shiitake mushroom, soaked in hot water for 15 minutes
1 tablespoon potato starch
2 tablespoons sake
1½ tablespoons soy sauce
1 tablespoon mirin
1 teaspoon caster (superfine) sugar
1 egg, whisked
300 g (10½ oz) minced (ground) chicken
1 spring onion (scallion), finely sliced
1 tablespoon aka miso (red miso paste)
2 teaspoons poppy seeds

Preheat the oven to 170°C (340°F). Line a 15 cm (6 in) square baking dish with baking paper.

Finely chop the rehydrated shiitake.

In a bowl, mix the potato starch, sake, soy sauce, mirin and sugar until smooth.

Reserve 1 tablespoon of the whisked egg. In a bowl, combine the remaining egg with the chicken meat and mix vigorously until sticky and well combined. Add the shiitake and spring onion, mix well, then add the starch mixture and mix until fully homogeneous.

Spread the mixture evenly in the baking dish, smoothing the surface so the mixture is about 2–3 cm (¾–1¼ in) thick. Bake for 20 minutes.

Brush with the reserved egg, sprinkle with the poppy seeds and bake for another 5 minutes, or until a skewer inserted into the centre of the loaf comes out hot.

Remove from the oven and cool completely before cutting into nine larger pieces, or 16 bite-sized portions.

Store refrigerated for up to 4 days, or freeze for up to 1 month.

TORINIKU NO NARUTO

Serves 1 as a main
or 4 in an ekiben

NARUTO-STYLE ROLLED CHICKEN・鶏肉の鳴門巻き

Chicken breast rolled with umeboshi (pickled plum) and shiso leaves is a familiar dish in home kitchens and izakaya across Japan. While this version is coated in tempura batter, it can also be crumbed with panko and fried, or simply pan-grilled.

'Naruto' means 'whirlpool', referring to the spiral pattern created by the plum and shiso when the chicken is sliced.

- 100 g (3½ oz) tempura flour, plus extra for dusting
- 150 ml (5 fl oz) cold water
- 1 egg yolk
- 1 chicken breast
- salt
- 1 tablespoon ume paste (pickled plum paste)
- 2 shiso leaves
- 1 litre (4 cups) neutral oil

Place the flour, water and egg yolk in separate bowls and transfer to the fridge to chill thoroughly before use.

Using a sharp knife, slice the chicken breast in half horizontally, then open each half out like a book. The meat should be less than 1 cm (½ in) thick. Lightly season with salt and dust with tempura flour.

With the long edge of the chicken facing you, spread the ume paste lightly over the lower three-quarters of the chicken and cover the ume with shiso leaves. Roll the chicken up tightly from the long edge and secure with toothpicks.

In a deep, heavy-based pan, heat the oil to 175°C (345°F).

Meanwhile, make the batter. Whisk the egg yolk into the cold water, then sift in the flour, whisking gently until just combined. The batter should be thin and lightly lumpy; add more water if needed.

Dust the rolled chicken lightly with tempura flour, then coat in the batter and gently lower into the oil. Using chopsticks, drizzle a little extra batter over the chicken to create a craggy, crisp texture. Fry for 6–7 minutes, turning occasionally and skimming off the stray batter, until the chicken is hot through.

Carefully remove the chicken from the oil. Drain on paper towel, season with salt and allow to cool slightly. Take out the toothpicks, then slice and serve.

The chicken can be prepared a day ahead and refrigerated.

TOTTORI

Located on the northwestern coast of Japan's largest island, Honshu, the prefecture of Tottori is perhaps best known for its sand dunes – an unexpected sight in a country more often associated with forests, mountains and streams. Stretching along the Sea of Japan coast about 30 minutes north of Tottori Station, the dunes are modest by global standards, but still striking and worth visiting, especially if you're looking for a change of scene from waterfalls and alpine trails.

Tottori's waters provide an abundance of seafood, particularly shellfish such as crab, prawns (shrimp) and oysters. Snow crab, in particular, is a regional pride, celebrated in winter and showcased in ekiben such as San'in Tottori Kanimeshi.

For those wanting something different, Tottori also has a strong ramen culture. Gyukotsu ramen (beef-bone ramen) is a local specialty. Beef bones are simmered into a clear, deeply flavoured broth and served with chashu (braised pork belly), ajitama (soy-marinated ramen egg), bean sprouts and negi (long green onion). It's a hearty reminder that Tottori's food culture extends well beyond the sea.

TOTTORI PREFECTURE

Tottori Station, Tottori・鳥取駅、鳥取県

35.5192° N, 134.2004° E

SAN'IN TOTTORI KANIMESHI

Tottori snow crab rice・山陰鳥取かにめし

A show-stopping ekiben filled with snow crab, presented in a distinctive, eye-catching box that is, fittingly, shaped like a crab. This is one of Japan's more expensive ekiben, but once opened, it's immediately clear that it is worth the expense. The crab meat is painstakingly hand-picked, with two whole, meaty claws placed prominently on top as a centrepiece. Beneath them, the rice is lightly seasoned with kani miso – the rich innards of the crab – which gives the bento a deep, savoury seafood flavour, without overwhelming the palate.

First created in 1952, this ekiben is produced by Abe Tottorido, a company founded in 1910 and known for specialising in Tottori ingredients and regional preparations. Their catalogue includes squid and squid-ink rice (Ika sumi bento kuromeshi), as well as mackerel (San'in Tottori zeitakuna ippin saba sushi) and flying fish sushi (San'in Tottori ago sushi).

The word 'San'in' refers to the region along the Sea of Japan coast of western Honshu. It includes Tottori and Shimane prefectures, along with parts of northern Yamaguchi, Kyoto and Okayama. Though less densely populated than the Pacific side of Japan, San'in has outsized historical importance. It is closely associated with the origins of Shinto mythology, and was once a powerful cultural centre with early maritime links to China and Korea.

Opening the lid

1. ZUWAIGANI

Tender flakes of sweet, juicy snow crab meat. The two claws are carefully removed whole and placed on top for a dramatic, satisfying bite.

2. GOHAN (PAGE 22)

Rice lightly mixed with kani miso (crab innards), giving it a subtle crab richness that amplifies the flavour of the seafood that sits on top.

3. FUKUJINZUKE

Radish pickled in sweet soy sauce and vinegar. Commonly served with Japanese curry, it makes a surprising appearance here. This may be a nod to Tottori's famously high curry consumption – the highest per capita in Japan.

博多長浜
ラーメン
大ちゃん
おでん
牛タン
串焼
ラーメン
焼ラーメン
もつ焼
おでん
焼とり
酒処
やきとり
ラーメン
TOWER

FUKUOKA

Blessed with a temperate climate year-round, Fukuoka is one of Japan's most liveable and rewarding food cities. It offers the breadth of dining found in Tokyo or Osaka, but without the same intensity of crowds. In the evenings, riverside streets come alive with yatai – open-air food stalls that are now rare outside of festivals elsewhere in Japan. Pull up a stool and you might find grilled meats, motsunabe (beef offal hotpot), oden (hearty one-pot stew of skewered meat, vegetables and fish cakes) or late-night ramen.

Despite the warmer weather, Fukuoka is the birthplace of Japan's richest ramen style: tonkotsu ramen. Pork bones are boiled continuously until the broth turns milky white from emulsified fat, producing a soup that is deep, savoury and creamy. Ramen lovers from all over the world make the pilgrimage here to try the original tonkotsu ramen from Nankin Senryo, and the many other shops there that have since evolved their own unique recipes and styles.

FUKUOKA PREFECTURE

Hakata Station, Fukuoka・博多駅、福岡県

33.5900° N, 130.4199° E

KASHIWA-MESHI

Chicken rice・かしわめし

Presented in a beautiful old-style box with a nostalgic label, Kashiwa-Meshi is one of Fukuoka's (and the island of Kyushu's) most recognisable ekiben. 'Kashiwa' is the local dialect word for 'chicken', and kashiwa-meshi is a dish unique to the region, traditionally made with Hakata chicken, a breed that is prized for its deep, savoury flavour.

The preparation is simple but carefully balanced. Chicken is chopped and simmered, and the rice is cooked in the same broth, absorbing the richness and flavour of the meat. Once cooked, the rice is topped with chicken, kinshi tamago (page 27) and nori seaweed, arranged in clean, separate lines that give Kashiwa-Meshi its distinctive appearance.

The three colours – brown, yellow and black – are a key visual element of the dish. Variations may substitute hijiki or other seaweed for nori, or use softly scrambled egg in place of kinshi tamago, but the emphasis on contrast remains.

This particular ekiben label is a reproduction of a design said to date back to the 1940s, reinforcing its connection to Kyushu's railway dining history.

Opening the lid

1. KASHIWA (PAGE 196)

Local chicken that is boiled, roughly chopped with the skin on, lightly fried in sesame oil, then simmered with vegetables such as carrot, shiitake and burdock root. This mixture is then seasoned with sake, mirin and soy sauce.

2. GOHAN (PAGE 22)

The rice component of this ekiben is cooked in the broth from boiling the chicken, giving it a gentle savoury flavour and pale brown colour. Simpler versions use plain white rice, adding the already cooked chicken towards the end before mixing everything together.

3. KINSHI TAMAGO (PAGE 27) AND NORI

Finely shredded egg and nori complete the three-colour composition, bringing together Kyushu's chicken culture and its long tradition of seaweed production.

4. HIJIKI (PAGE 197)

A fine, black seaweed with earthy, oceanic notes, stir-fried, then simmered in soy-flavoured stock until gently chewy and umami-rich.

5. TSUKEMONO (PAGE 197)

Daikon and carrot pickled in kombu-infused amazu vinegar, sweet and sour with added depth from shredded seaweed.

RECIPES ➡

KASHIWA-MESHI

Serves 4

CHICKEN RICE・かしわめし

This recipe is a variation of the Kashiwa-Meshi ekiben that includes additional vegetables, reflecting the home-style versions of kashiwa-meshi that are commonly cooked throughout households on the island of Kyushu.

Keeping the skin on the chicken thigh is a distinctive feature of this dish. The skin gives more aroma to the broth, and is also said to provide more flavour as you chew, as the slight resistance allows you to chew it for longer.

- 300 g (10½ oz) boneless chicken thighs, skin on
- 600 g (1 lb 5 oz) short-grain white rice
- 1 tablespoon sesame oil
- ½ carrot, julienned
- 4 dried shiitake mushrooms, soaked in hot water for 10 minutes, then sliced
- 80 g (½ cup) julienned burdock root (optional)
- 60 ml (¼ cup) soy sauce
- 60 ml (¼ cup) sake
- 2 tablespoons mirin
- 1 tablespoon caster (superfine) sugar
- 1 cup kinshi tamago (page 27), approx. 100 g (3½ oz)
- 10 g (½ cup) kizami nori (shredded nori)

BROTH

- 1 litre (4 cups) chicken stock, dashi (page 23) or water
- 2 tablespoons sake
- 1 tablespoon soy sauce
- 1 thumb-sized piece ginger, sliced

In a saucepan, bring the broth ingredients to the boil. Reduce the heat to a simmer and add the chicken thighs. Simmer for 15 minutes, or until just cooked through, then remove the chicken.

Strain the broth and reserve 625 ml (2½ cups) for cooking the rice, and 125 ml (½ cup) for finishing the chicken.

Wash the rice until the water runs clear.

Place the washed rice in a donabe, lidded saucepan or rice cooker along with the 625 ml reserved broth (or enough liquid to reach the level recommended by the rice cooker manufacturer). Follow the instructions on page 22 to soak and cook the rice with the reserved broth.

Meanwhile, roughly chop the cooled chicken into pebble-sized pieces.

Heat a large frying pan over medium heat and add the sesame oil. Add the chicken and cook until all the moisture evaporates. Add the carrot, shiitake and burdock root, if using, and stir-fry for 3–5 minutes, until the vegetables are just tender.

Add the soy sauce, sake, mirin, sugar and the remaining 125 ml of the reserved broth. Bring to the boil, then simmer for 5 minutes. Remove from the heat and allow to cool, then strain, reserving the braising liquid.

Once the rice is cooked, gently fold the reserved braising liquid through.

Pack the rice into bento boxes or on plates and arrange the chicken mixture, kinshi tamago and kizami nori in clean lines across the top.

Once assembled, the dish will keep refrigerated for up to 2 days.

HIJIKI

ひじき

Serves 2

Hijiki is a soft seaweed that retains its texture long after cooking, making it ideal for including in bento. It is often used in salads and simmered dishes.

Hijiki can be difficult to find outside Japan, as some countries advise against its sale because it absorbs higher levels of arsenic compared to other seaweed varieties. In Japan, it is considered safe when eaten in small quantities as part of a varied diet. Dried wood ear mushrooms make a good substitute if you want to avoid hijiki or if it's unavailable.

- 15 g (½ oz) dried hijiki or wood ear mushrooms
- 1 tablespoon neutral oil
- 125 ml (½ cup) dashi (page 23)
- 2 tablespoons soy sauce
- 1 tablespoon mirin
- 1 tablespoon caster (superfine) sugar

Place the dried hijiki in a heatproof bowl, cover with hot water and leave to rehydrate for 15 minutes. Drain, discarding the soaking liquid.

Heat the oil in a saucepan over medium heat. Add the hijiki and stir-fry for 1 minute, until dry.

Add the remaining ingredients and bring to the boil, then simmer for 5–8 minutes, until most of the liquid has evaporated.

Cool and refrigerate until needed. The hijiki keeps for up to 4 days refrigerated, or 1 month frozen.

DAIKON TO KOMBU NO AMAZU-ZUKE

Makes about 250 g (1 cup)

SWEET VINEGAR PICKLED DAIKON AND KOMBU・大根と昆布の甘酢漬け

At its simplest, this is daikon cut into neat slices and lightly pickled in sweetened vinegar, often with slivers of kombu. The result is crisp, clean and gently sweet–sour, with a savoury undertone from the seaweed. Citrus peel, most commonly yuzu, can be substituted for kombu for a brighter finish.

- 300 g (10½ oz) daikon
- 1 tablespoon salt
- 5 cm (2 in) piece kombu

BRINE

- 230 ml (8 fl oz) water
- 80 g (⅓ cup) caster (superfine) sugar
- 1 tablespoon salt
- 130 ml (4½ fl oz) rice vinegar

To make the brine, bring the water, sugar and salt to a simmer in a small saucepan until the sugar and salt dissolve. Remove from the heat, add the vinegar and leave to cool.

Peel the daikon, cut into quarters, then slice into 5 mm (¼ in) thick triangles. Toss with the salt until the liquid releases. Squeeze out the excess liquid, and drain in a sieve.

Cut the kombu into thin strips. Place in a non-reactive container with the daikon. Pour the cooled brine over, and weigh down with a plate to submerge the daikon.

Cover and marinate in the fridge for at least 3 days; the pickle will keep refrigerated for up to 1 month.

INTERVIEW WITH
HASHIMA TOMOYUKI

'You opened the train window, leaned your head out, and they handed you an ekiben. That was the joy of travel.'

A LIFE IN PRINT

I found Mr Hashima Tomoyuki through a book he authored called *A Comprehensive Guide to Ekiben Labels from the Meiji, Taisho, and Showa Eras.* It's a beautiful and rare book containing hundreds of images from Mr Hashima's collection, with anecdotes about the times the labels came from, and how changing technology and circumstances are reflected in ekiben labels. Reading it, I felt an irresistible urge to meet the person who had assembled such a remarkable archive.

Hashima Tomoyuki has spent most of his life collecting paper: newspapers, advertisements, labels and other fragments of everyday life that most people throw away without a second thought. What began as a high school hobby grew into a vast private archive that includes one of the most extensive collections of ekiben labels in Japan. Now in his nineties, Mr Hashima speaks less like a collector guarding a legacy and more like a witness quietly taking stock.

Q: *COULD YOU PLEASE INTRODUCE YOURSELF AND HOW YOU STARTED COLLECTING EKIBEN LABELS?*

A:

I was born in Tokyo in 1935. Just after [World War II], when I was in the second year of junior high school, my Japanese teacher talked to us about newspapers – how to read them, how to think about them. That stayed with me. I started collecting them then. By the time I was a university student, I already had around 25,000 items. That collection later became the foundation of the Japan Newspaper Museum in Yokohama. It covers newspapers from the end of the Edo period through the Meiji, Taisho and Showa periods, including woodblock-printed news sheets.

Once you start collecting one thing, it never stays as one thing. It expands. Newspapers led to advertisements. Advertisements led to labels. Labels led to ekiben.

One day I was walking through a secondhand bookstore in Kanda. They used to sell all kinds of paper there – documents, scraps, things people didn't know how to value. Mixed in to the pile were ekiben labels. I bought a few without really knowing why. Later, someone offered to sell me a whole collection of labels. It was very expensive for the time. I don't even remember the exact reason why I agreed. When you collect, sometimes your hand moves before your head does.

Q: *WHAT WERE EKIBEN LIKE WHEN YOU WERE GROWING UP?*

A:

That's difficult to say. In the early Showa era, there weren't many ekiben at all. People usually brought food from home — rice balls, inari sushi, maybe bread. Ekiben were small, simple. They were good quality, but the real issue was freshness – there was no way to keep food cool. If you bought one, you had to eat it quickly. If someone got food poisoning, the seller was responsible. That's why sellers were always shouting for people to buy and eat ekiben immediately.

Q: *HOW WERE EKIBEN SOLD BACK THEN?*

A:

When the train stopped, people opened the windows. Everyone leaned out at once. Sellers ran along the platform with baskets, shouting. You had maybe five minutes to buy the ekiben. If you missed it, that was it – no food until the next station. The train windows don't open now. That alone tells you how much has changed.

Q: *WHAT MAKES EKIBEN UNIQUELY JAPANESE?*

A:

The idea of eating local food every time a train arrives – that way of thinking feels very Japanese. Each region has its own character. Trout sushi, eel rice, clams, mountain vegetables. You learned geography through taste. Travel took time. Tokyo to Osaka was ten hours. You *had* to eat along the way.

Q: *HOW DID WARTIME AFFECT EKIBEN?*

A:

During the war, ekiben were almost impossible to find. You needed meal coupons to buy them. People ate sweet potatoes, potatoes, radishes. Rice was precious.

Ekiben labels from that era sometimes carried propaganda (see page 201) – slogans about saving money, supporting the nation. I included some of that material in a book about wartime life. Ekiben reflect the times very clearly.

Q: *WHAT MAKES A GOOD EKIBEN LABEL?*

A:

Rarity, not beauty alone. Labels from stations where only a few trains stopped each day are especially valuable. Fewer passengers meant fewer ekiben were sold, so fewer labels survive.

Some ekiben were sold with two tiers – rice in one box, side dishes in another. Those were called joto ekiben. They were more expensive.

Q: *HOW DO YOU FEEL ABOUT EKIBEN TODAY?*

A:

Ekiben are very expensive now. They used to be cheap – 30 sen (about 300 yen today). Now they're full of crab, sea urchin, luxury ingredients. People buy them at department stores and take them home. There's even an ekiben 'department store' at Tokyo Station (page 74, pictured below). That's fine, times change.

But back then, ekiben were a necessity. You ate because you were travelling. Now train travel is too fast. By the time you open the ekiben, you've arrived at your destination.

Q: *DO YOU STILL COLLECT?*

A:

No, not really. I'm in my nineties, and I forget things. Sometimes I open a box of labels or papers and don't remember when I bought them, or why. I take something out, look at it, and put it back. Collecting is a human instinct, but even instincts get tired.

Q: *IS THERE ANYTHING YOU'D LIKE READERS TO UNDERSTAND?*

A:

Ekiben aren't special by themselves. They mattered because travel took time. You waited. You were hungry. You leaned out the window. That waiting was part of the journey. Now the windows don't open. The trains don't stop. The platforms are quiet.

That's not good or bad. It's just the era we live in.

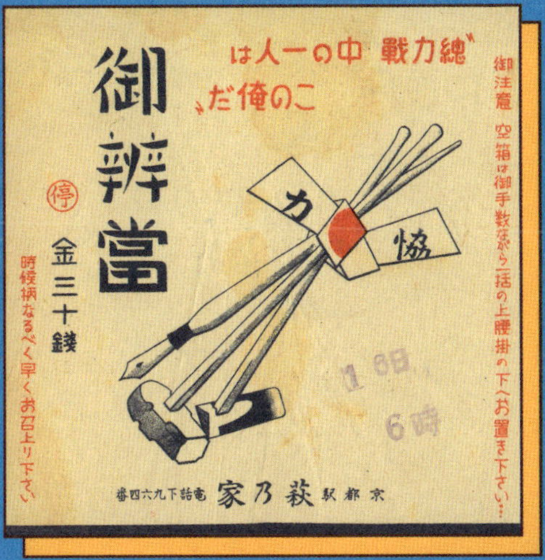

Credit: The Railway Museum

Left: *During the early stages of the war, ekiben packaging became a vehicle for morale. This label replaces familiar images of scenery with slogans and symbols: bundled tools marked 'strength' and 'cooperation' and text asserting that national power resided in the people themselves.*

Consumption was framed as a disciplined act, with instructions urging restraint, order and consideration for wartime conditions as everyday life in Japan was mobilised for total war.

This ekiben label from Kyoto includes the phrase: 'Total War strength lies within the people – but it begins with each of us.'

Right: *A rare label noted by Mr Hashima in his book. This ekiben label was sold in colonial Korea at Shoyomon Station (present-day Seoul) and depicts the Peiping Gate – today known as Zhengyangmen in Beijing.*

Issued after Japan's occupation of Beijing in 1937, the label reflects how ekiben imagery was used to project imperial geography, linking rail travel, food and newly conquered territory.

Credit: The Railway Museum

Credit: The Railway Museum

Left: *By 1944, ekiben packaging had become starkly utilitarian.*

This wartime label from Itoigawa uses stamped text alone to record place, price and point-of-sale preparation, with no imagery or product name.

Printed on coarse paper and sold at a fixed price under rationing, it reflects how ekiben shifted from souvenir to regulated necessity in the final years of the war.

FUKUOKA PREFECTURE

Hakata Station, Fukuoka · 博多駅、福岡県

33.5900° N, 130.4199° E

HAKATA NO AJI YAMAYA KARASHI MENTAIKO TO NISHU DARE TONBARA BENTO

Hakata's Taste Yamaya spicy mentaiko and pork belly bento with two sauces
博多の味やまや辛子明太子と二種だれ豚バラ弁当

Another specialty of Fukuoka Prefecture is mentaiko, or spicy cod roe. Mentaiko is made by curing cod roe in sake, dashi and red pepper flakes. Despite the use of chilli, most mentaiko is very mild and can be enjoyed even by those who avoid spicy food.

In Fukuoka, entire shops are devoted to mentaiko, selling it fresh, as a paste or flavoured into crackers (senbei), and even soft-serve ice cream. The city's affection for mentaiko is unmistakable, and many ekiben feature it prominently. If you can find mentaiko at an Asian grocers, it's excellent simply served over rice or enjoyed as ochazuke (a comforting soup). One of its most popular uses nationwide is mentaiko pasta: buttered spaghetti mixed with roe, a touch of soy sauce, and finished with shredded nori.

This bento celebrates the region's signature mentaiko alongside Fukuoka pork, prepared with two contrasting sauces – one savoury and one spicy.

Opening the lid

1. MENTAIKO

The star of the bento, spicy cod roe, sits proudly at the centre, dusted with chilli flakes. Salty and gently spicy, it pairs effortlessly with every other element.

2. FUKUOKA BUTA (PAGE 204)

Fukuoka's local pork ('buta' means 'pork') is prized for its sweet, clean fat and tender texture. Fukuoka's love of pork is evident in dishes like tonkotsu ramen and motsunabe, a miso- or soy-based offal hotpot topped with garlic chives that tastes far better than it sounds. Yakitori and yakiton are also popular, and the pork in this ekiben echoes those familiar flavours. Edamame provides a light, refreshing counterpoint to the richness.

3. KYABETSU

Kyabetsu – cabbage – is a surprising but very Hakata addition. Often served alongside pork dishes, it adds crunch and is said to soften the fattiness of the meat. Yakitori restaurants commonly serve cabbage dressed with ponzu, placing grilled skewers directly on top so the juices soak in. Many offer unlimited refills to cleanse the palate – and encourage another order.

4. YUDE TAMAGO

A simply boiled egg offers a neutral pause between bites of marinated pork and mentaiko.

5. DAIKON AMAZU-ZUKE (PAGE 197)

Sweet-and-sour pickled daikon adds crunch and acidity to balance the richness of the bento.

RECIPES ➡

BUTABARA-YAKI

Serves 2

GRILLED PORK BELLY・豚バラ焼き

Reflecting Fukuoka's ramen culture, the region places great importance on tare, or seasoning sauces. Each ramen shop guards its own recipe, blending soy- or salt-based sauces with seafood and aromatics to create distinctive flavours. This recipe aims to capture that spirit.

Inspired by the popularity of grilled meat across the prefecture, this dish uses two classic seasonings: shio (salt-based) and amakara (sweet and savoury). These sauces can also be brushed onto skewers for a barbecue if you prefer.

2 cabbage leaves
75 g (½ cup) raw edamame (fresh or frozen)
2 tablespoons neutral oil
200 g (7 oz) boneless pork belly, sliced 5 mm (¼ in) thick and cut into 5 cm (2 in) lengths
steamed rice (page 22), to serve
2 mentaiko (spicy cod roe) lobes

AMAKARA TARE

1 tablespoon soy sauce
1 tablespoon caster (superfine) sugar
1 tablespoon mirin
1 tablespoon sake
1 tablespoon rice vinegar
1 tablespoon water
½ teaspoon dashi powder

SHIO TARE

2 tablespoons sake
1 tablespoon sesame oil
1 tablespoon water
½ teaspoon salt
½ teaspoon caster (superfine) sugar
½ teaspoon dashi powder
1 garlic clove, minced
ground black pepper, to taste

Bring a saucepan of lightly salted water to the boil. Blanch the cabbage leaves for 1 minute, until just softened; remove, cool and cut into bite-sized pieces. In the same water, blanch the edamame for 2 minutes. Drain, cool in cold water, then remove from their pods. Set aside.

To prepare the sauces, mix the amakara tare ingredients in one small bowl, and the shio tare ingredients in another small bowl.

Heat 1 tablespoon of the oil in a frying pan over high heat. Add half the pork belly in a single layer and cook until well coloured on both sides. Reduce the heat to low, then add the shio tare. Cook for about 5 minutes, turning the pork, until the sauce has reduced by half and the pork is cooked through. Remove the pork to a bowl.

Wipe out the pan, heat the remaining oil, and repeat with the remaining pork and the amakara tare.

To assemble, layer the rice in the bento, followed by the cabbage. Place the mentaiko in the centre. Arrange the shio-flavoured pork on one side and the amakara pork on the other, then scatter the edamame over the top.

Once assembled, the dish will keep refrigerated for 1 day.

島原港
ワンマン
V-VAREN
NAGASAKI
V・ファーレン長崎 × 島原鉄道株式会社

NAGASAKI

Often defined by its tragic past, Nagasaki today is a lively, beautiful port city. During Japan's period of isolation, it was the country's sole point of contact with the outside world, the only port where foreign trade was permitted. That history shaped a cuisine unlike any other in Japan.

Dishes such as champon (noodle soup) and sara udon (crispy fried noodles, page 210) blend Chinese techniques with Japanese ingredients, creating food that feels both foreign and familiar. Portuguese traders introduced castella (page 232), a light yet rich sponge cake scented with honey, which has since become beloved nationwide.

Surrounded by sheltered bays and fertile fishing grounds, Nagasaki enjoys abundant seafood. Nagasaki bluefin tuna is among the most prized in Japan, alongside squid, shellfish and coastal fish that appear across the city's menus.

NAGASAKI PREFECTURE

Nagasaki Station, Nagasaki・長崎駅、長崎県

32.7524° N, 129.8689° E

NAGASAKI CHUKA BENTO TSUBAKI

Nagasaki Chinese cuisine camellia・長崎中華弁当つばき

Another region shaped by strong Chinese influences, Nagasaki is home to one of Japan's most distinctive noodle dishes: Sara udon. A generous mix of meat, seafood and colourful fish cakes is cloaked in a thick, flavoursome sauce and poured over crisp, fried noodles.

The noodles themselves are unique – they are thin, made of wheat and have been fried until brittle and crunchy, not unlike deep-fried instant noodles. Even when coated in sauce, they retain their texture remarkably well, staying crisp rather than soggy. The result is a dish that recalls chow mein, yet remains satisfyingly crunchy even when cold. It's comforting and utterly moreish, and anyone visiting Nagasaki should make a point of seeking it out.

Opening the lid

1. SARA UDON (PAGE 210)

The centrepiece of the bento. Despite being pre-packaged and reheated, the noodles remain crisp and textural.

2. HARUMAKI (PAGE 212)

Spring rolls filled with finely sliced pork and vegetables in a sweet-savoury sauce.

3. KARAAGE (PAGE 98)

Soy-marinated, crispy-crumbed fried chicken is always welcome in a bento!

4. CHINJAO ROSU (PAGE 214)

Shredded pork that has been stir-fried with green bell pepper (capsicum). This dish has a strong soy flavour, which makes it an interesting counterpoint to the lighter dishes in the ekiben.

5. KAISEN TO YASAI NO SHIO ITAME (PAGE 215)

A lightly seasoned stir-fry of seafood and vegetables in a gently thickened broth. Similar in method to the sara udon topping, but using different ingredients such as squid, clams, bamboo shoots, bell pepper (capsicum) and broccoli which have been neatly arranged.

6. GOHAN (PAGE 22)

Steamed rice that has been simply sprinkled with black sesame seeds.

RECIPES ➡

SARA UDON

Serves 4

'PLATE' UDON・皿うどん

Sara udon can be thought of as the 'dry' cousin to champon, Nagasaki's famous noodle soup created at Shikairo, a restaurant that has been operating in the city since 1899. While champon uses ramen-style noodles that have been simmered in a chicken and pork broth, sara udon replaces them with crisp, fried noodles cut into short lengths. These are then topped with seafood, meat and vegetables that have been cooked in a glossy, thick sauce.

In Nagasaki, ready-made sara udon noodles are sold in most supermarkets. Outside Japan, fried instant ramen noodles work well as a substitute. One excellent alternative is sapo mee, a Malaysian fried noodle with long strands that can be heated in the oven to re-crisp them, before being lightly crushed.

The proteins and vegetables are flexible and can be adjusted to what's available, but onion and carrot are important for building flavour and sweetness in the sauce, and kamaboko (pink-ringed fish cake) is essential for colour and texture.

- 8 quail eggs
- 2 tablespoons sesame oil
- 100 g (3½ oz) pork tenderloin, cut into thin strips
- 100 g (3½ oz) fresh scallops, without roe
- 100 g (3½ oz) prawns (shrimp), peeled and deveined
- 2 cabbage leaves, cut into 2 cm (¾ in) squares
- ½ carrot, julienned
- ½ onion, sliced
- 2 fresh shiitake mushrooms, stems removed, sliced
- 1 tablespoon sake
- 50 g (1¾ oz) bean sprouts
- 6 cm (2½ in) piece kamaboko (about 75 g/2¾ oz), cut into 5 mm (¼ in) thick slices
- 1 bunch choy sum (Chinese flowering cabbage), cut into 5 cm (2 in) lengths
- 4 serves sara udon (pre-fried ready-to-eat noodles)

SAUCE

- 400 ml (14 fl oz) chicken stock or water
- 1 teaspoon chicken stock powder
- 2 tablespoons potato starch
- 1 tablespoon oyster sauce
- 1 tablespoon sake
- 2 teaspoons soy sauce
- ½ teaspoon ground white pepper

To hard boil the quail eggs, bring a saucepan of water to the boil. Meanwhile, prepare a bowl of iced water. Add the quail eggs to the boiling water and cook for 4 minutes.

Transfer to the iced water and set aside to cool. Peel the quail eggs and reserve.

Mix together the sauce ingredients and set aside.

Heat 1 tablespoon of the sesame oil in a frying pan over medium heat. Fry the pork for about 5 minutes – stirring occasionally. Once the pork has changed colour and is cooked through, add the scallops and prawns. Fry for a further 2 minutes, or until the seafood is just cooked, then remove from the pan.

Heat the remaining sesame oil in the pan and add the cabbage, carrot, onion and shiitake. Mix to combine, then pour in the sake and cook for about 2 minutes, until the vegetables have softened.

Return the cooked pork and seafood to the pan, as well as the bean sprouts. Mix well, add the sauce and cook for a further 1 minute, or until thickened.

Finally, add the kamaboko, quail eggs and choy sum. Cook for another minute or two, until the choy sum is wilted and everything is hot.

If eating immediately, distribute the sara udon between plates and top with the stir-fry sauce.

Alternatively, allow to cool to room temperature, place the sara udon in bentos, then pour over the cooled sauce.

Once assembled, the bentos will keep refrigerated for 1 day.

HARUMAKI

Makes 10

PORK SPRING ROLLS・春巻き

The key to these spring rolls is cutting all the ingredients into fine strips, ensuring each bite is cohesive and easy to eat. A rich oyster sauce ties everything together.

Feel free to replace the pork with chicken breast, beef tenderloin, or, for a vegetarian option, replace the meat with bell pepper (capsicum) and substitute the oyster sauce for a vegan version and omit the chicken stock powder.

- 2 dried shiitake mushrooms
- 1 tablespoon sesame oil
- 100 g (3½ oz) pork tenderloin, julienned
- ½ onion, julienned
- ½ carrot, julienned
- 50 g (1¾ oz) fresh wood ear mushrooms, julienned
- 1 spring onion (scallion), finely sliced
- 1 tablespoon plain (all-purpose) flour
- 10 square spring roll wrappers, 21.5 cm (8½ in) in size
- neutral oil, for deep-frying

SAUCE

- 100 ml (3½ fl oz) shiitake soaking water (see method)
- 2 tablespoons oyster sauce
- 2 tablespoons soy sauce
- 1 tablespoon mirin
- 1 tablespoon caster (superfine) sugar
- 1 teaspoon chicken stock powder
- ½ teaspoon grated ginger
- ½ teaspoon potato starch
- pinch of ground white pepper

Place the dried shiitake in a heatproof bowl, cover with hot water and leave to rehydrate for 30 minutes. Drain, reserving 100 ml (3½ fl oz) of the soaking liquid. Slice the mushrooms finely.

Mix together the sauce ingredients (including the reserved shiitake soaking water).

Heat a large frying pan over medium–high heat and add the sesame oil. Stir-fry the pork, onion, carrot and shiitake and wood ear mushrooms for about 3 minutes, until the pork is coloured.

Add the sauce and cook over high heat for another 3 minutes, until the sauce has thickened and mostly evaporated. Mix in the spring onion and allow to cool.

Mix the flour to a smooth slurry with 2 tablespoons water.

Place a spring roll wrapper on your work surface with a point facing towards you. Place a heaped tablespoon of the filling in the centre of the bottom half of the wrapper. Moisten the edges lightly with some of the flour slurry. Fold the bottom over the filling, then fold in the sides. Roll up tightly from the bottom and seal with more of the flour slurry.

Repeat with the remaining wrappers and filling. (Any spring rolls you don't wish to fry straight away can be placed on baking paper in an airtight container and cooked the next day, or they can be frozen for up to 1 week.)

In a deep heavy-based saucepan or deep-fryer, heat about 5 cm (2 in) of oil to 180°C (350°F).

Fry the spring rolls in batches for 5 minutes, or until golden, turning them over halfway. Drain on a wire rack and serve straight away, or refrigerate and enjoy the next day.

CHINJAO ROSU

Serves 2 as a main with rice, or 4 as part of a shared meal

GREEN PEPPER STIR-FRY・青椒肉絲

Chinjao rosu is a boldly flavoured stir-fry that is defined by uniform cutting. All the ingredients are sliced into similar shapes, ensuring quick, even cooking and a pleasing texture.

This recipe makes for an excellent weeknight dinner, served simply with rice.

- 300 g (10½ oz) beef or pork loin, cut into strips about 1 cm (½ in) wide
- 2 tablespoons sake
- 1 teaspoon potato starch
- 1 tablespoon neutral oil
- 1 tablespoon sesame oil
- ½ bell pepper (capsicum), red or green (or a mix of both), cut into strips
- 225 g (8 oz) tin bamboo shoots, drained and cut into strips

SAUCE

- 2 teaspoons grated ginger
- 2 garlic cloves, peeled and grated
- 2 tablespoons oyster sauce
- 2 tablespoons shaoxing wine
- 1 tablespoon caster (superfine) sugar
- 2 teaspoons chicken stock powder
- 2 teaspoons soy sauce
- 2 teaspoons mirin
- 2 teaspoons chu hou sauce (see Note)

In a small bowl, mix together the sauce ingredients.

In a separate bowl, mix together the meat, sake and potato starch.

In a frying pan, heat the neutral and sesame oils over medium heat. Stir-fry the meat for about 5 minutes, until coloured.

Add the bell pepper and bamboo shoots and stir-fry for another 2 minutes, or until the bell pepper is just cooked.

Stir the sauce through. Cook for another 3 minutes, or until the sauce bubbles and coats the meat and vegetables.

Remove from the heat. Serve immediately, or allow to cool, then refrigerate; keeps for 1 day.

NOTE //

The sauce uses chu hou sauce, which is a Cantonese condiment that is often used in braised meat and vegetable dishes. Chu hou sauce is made with fermented soybeans, garlic, ginger, sesame seeds and Chinese five-spice powder. It may be substituted with hoisin or tianmianjiang (sweet bean sauce) depending on your preference.

KAISEN TO YASAI NO SHIO ITAME

Serves 2 as a main with rice, or 4 as part of a shared meal

SEAFOOD AND VEGETABLES STIR-FRIED WITH SALT・海鮮と野菜の塩炒め

Light seasoning allows the sweetness of seafood to shine in this dish. With no soy sauce, the flavour remains clean and delicate, relying simply on salt and stock for depth.

You can substitute other seafood, such as prawns (shrimp), sliced fish or scallops. Green vegetables are essential for crunch and colour, so broccoli, asparagus or beans regularly appear.

2 squid tubes, beak, cartridge and innards removed
1 cup raw clam meat, about 100 g (3½ oz)
¼ head broccoli, cut into florets
225 g (8 oz) tin bamboo shoots, drained and finely sliced
2 tablespoons neutral oil
1 red bell pepper (capsicum), cut into 2 cm (¾ in) squares
1 cm (½ in) piece ginger, peeled and minced
1 garlic clove, minced

MARINADE

1 egg white, whisked
2 teaspoons sake
2 teaspoons potato starch
½ teaspoon salt
½ teaspoon ground white pepper

SAUCE

60 ml (¼ cup) chicken stock or water
1 tablespoon shaoxing wine
1 tablespoon sake
1 tablespoon potato starch
½ teaspoon chicken stock powder
½ teaspoon salt

In a bowl, mix together the marinade ingredients.

Using a sharp knife, slice the squid tubes open lengthways and lay them out flat, with the inside of the tubes facing up. Score all over in a criss-cross pattern, making a series of incisions about 5 mm (¼ in) apart – being careful not to cut all the way through.

Cut the squid into 2 cm (¾ in) squares, then add to the marinade with the clam meat. Mix well and allow to marinate for at least 5 minutes.

In a separate bowl, mix together the sauce ingredients and set aside.

Bring a saucepan of water to the boil and prepare a bowl of iced water. Blanch the broccoli and bamboo shoots for 3 minutes, then remove and refresh in the iced water.

Heat a large frying pan over medium heat, then add 1 tablespoon of the oil. Drain the seafood, discarding the marinade, and place in the pan in one layer. Cook for about 1 minute, until two-thirds cooked through. Flip the seafood over and cook for a further 30 seconds, then remove from the pan.

Wipe out the pan and add the remaining oil. Once heated, add the bell pepper, ginger, garlic, broccoli and bamboo shoots and stir-fry for 1 minute.

Return the seafood to the pan, then stir in the sauce. Mix well until thickened and immediately transfer to a plate.

Eat straight away, or allow to cool, arrange in bentos and refrigerate; keeps for 1 day.

MIYAZAKI

Set along Japan's southeastern edge, Miyazaki feels open and sunlit, a place where warmth shapes both landscape and attitude. At its centre is Miyazaki beef, one of Japan's most highly regarded wagyu regions. Raised with care on wide, green farmland, the beef is prized for its fine marbling and clean, sweet fat, and is usually served simply to let its quality speak without embellishment. Miyazaki and its neighbour, Kagoshima, are two of the top three largest wagyu producing prefectures, with Hokkaido completing the trio.

Mangoes – glowing orange and intensely sweet – round out the prefecture's image. Grown under careful conditions, they feel indulgent yet playful, a sunny counterpoint to the seriousness often associated with Japanese food culture.

Beyond the table, Miyazaki's spiritual heart lies in Takachiho Gorge. Sheer basalt cliffs frame emerald water, a setting deeply tied to Shinto mythology and the story of the sun goddess Amaterasu. A day here is spent immersed in nature, drifting through the gorge as waterfalls cascade beside you. The same spirit appears at lunch when eating nagashi somen (flowing noodles) – chilled noodles that have been served gently flowing down water in a hollowed-out bamboo chute, to be caught by diners' chopsticks and dunked in a savoury broth. A meal that is simple and nourishing for body and soul.

MIYAZAKI PREFECTURE

Miyazaki Station, Miyazaki · 宮崎駅、宮崎県

31.9158° N, 131.4320° E

MIYAZAKI CHIKIN NANBAN BENTO

Miyazaki chicken nanban bento · 宮崎チキン南蛮弁当

Chicken karaage may be Japan's most famous fried chicken, but chicken nanban might be the best suited to bento. The term 'nanban' refers to dishes inspired by Portuguese traders, who introduced new ingredients and techniques to Japan after they became shipwrecked on Tanegashima, an island south of Miyazaki. Their influence comes from the method of deep-frying and the use of sugar and vinegar in cooking, both techniques that are used in this recipe.

Unlike karaage, chicken nanban isn't prized for crispness – a quality that's largely lost once packed. Instead, chicken nanban uses a softer egg-and-flour batter. After frying, the chicken is soaked briefly in a sweet vinegar sauce, which is absorbed by this thicker coating while remaining intact, keeping the chicken moist and flavourful even when cooled. It is then served topped with tartar sauce, creating a rich yet balanced dish that travels exceptionally well.

Miyazaki is widely considered the birthplace of chicken nanban. Two local restaurants claim its invention: Nao-chan, which serves large chicken cutlets dressed only in the sweet-and-sour sauce, and Ogura, whose version includes tartar sauce and has become the more widely recognised style. Both are excellent, and each reflects a different interpretation of the same idea.

Opening the lid

1. SAKURAJIMA CHICKEN NANBAN (PAGE 220)

Fried chicken in a soft egg-and-flour batter. Sakurajima, a small peninsula in southern Kyushu, is home to an active volcano and lends its name to this prized local chicken, known for its tenderness and juiciness. Try the chicken on its own before adding the tartar sauce (page 221).

2. NAMUL

Korean-style seasoned bean sprouts, included in this bento as a reflection of the island of Kyushu's proximity to Korea. The namul adds crunch and a light sesame-soy flavour that contrasts with the rich chicken.

3. DASHIMAKI TAMAGO (PAGE 26)

Made with Miyazaki's highly regarded eggs, this rolled omelette is vibrant yellow, softly textured and gently sweet.

4. TAKANA

Pickled mustard greens, pleasantly salty and assertive. Kyushu is the origin of Japanese takana, so it's only fitting it appears in this bento.

5. SAKURA ZUKE DAIKON

Turnip, pickled in umeboshi vinegar, adds brightness, acidity and a light pink colour. The vegetable dishes provide contrast in flavour and texture, keeping the bento lively.

RECIPES ➡

CHICKEN NANBAN

Serves 4

SWEET AND SOUR FRIED CHICKEN・チキン南蛮

In this dish, the fried chicken is soaked briefly in a sweet and sour vinegar-based sauce, then topped generously with tartar sauce. It's rich, comforting and unapologetically bold, reflecting a local preference for food that satisfies deeply.

- 2 tablespoons caster (superfine) sugar
- 2 tablespoons salt
- 4 boneless chicken thighs, skin on
- neutral oil, for deep-frying
- 1 egg
- 50 g (⅓ cup) plain (all-purpose) flour
- 100 g (3½ oz) potato starch
- tartar sauce (opposite), to serve (optional)

SWEET AND SOUR SAUCE

- 80 ml (⅓ cup) water
- 80 ml (⅓ cup) mirin
- 40 ml (1¼ fl oz) soy sauce
- 2 tablespoons caster (superfine) sugar
- 1 garlic clove, peeled and minced
- 1 dried red chilli, deseeded and finely sliced
- 20 ml (¾ fl oz) rice vinegar
- 20 ml (¾ fl oz) lemon juice

In a large bowl, whisk together the sugar, salt and 1 litre (4 cups) water until the sugar and salt dissolve. Submerge the chicken thighs in the brine, then cover and refrigerate for 1 hour, to season the chicken and make it juicier.

To make the sweet and sour sauce, combine the water, mirin, soy sauce, sugar, garlic and chilli in a small saucepan. Bring to a gentle simmer, stirring until the sugar dissolves. Remove from the heat, then stir in the vinegar and lemon juice. Set aside.

In a deep heavy-based saucepan, heat about 5 cm (2 in) of oil to 160°C (320°F).

In a bowl, whisk the egg and flour with 30 ml (1 fl oz) water until smooth. Place the potato starch on a separate tray.

Drain the chicken, discarding the brine. Pat the chicken dry using paper towel, then coat in the egg mixture.

Working one piece at a time, remove the chicken from the egg mixture, allowing any excess to drip off, and coat thoroughly in the potato starch. Gently lower the chicken into the oil, taking care not to overcrowd the pot.

Fry for 4 minutes, turning halfway, until the coating has set. Remove and drain on a wire rack.

Once all the chicken has been fried, increase the oil temperature to 180°C (350°F) and fry again, in batches as needed, for 2–3 minutes, until golden brown and cooked through. Drain well.

While still hot, coat the chicken lightly in the sweet and sour sauce.

Serve straight away, topped with the tartar sauce, if you wish, or allow to cool, then refrigerate and enjoy the next day.

The chicken nanban will keep for up to 3 days.

KYUURI NO ASAZUKE

Makes about 250 ml (1 cup)

LIGHT PICKLED CUCUMBER・きゅうりの浅漬け

This pickle recipe is called asazuke (meaning 'light pickle') because it will be ready to eat on the same day it was prepared. This is a simple and versatile pickle that is perfect for many types of thinly sliced vegetables: cucumber, carrot, turnips, radishes or cabbage all work well.

- 3 short cucumbers
- salt
- 3 cm (1¼ in) piece kombu
- 1 tablespoon soy sauce
- 1 tablespoon mirin

Wash the cucumbers, dry thoroughly and cut into 5 mm (¼ in) slices. Weigh the sliced cucumbers at this stage, then place into a small bowl or container and add 2 per cent salt. (For example, if the cucumber slices weigh 100 g/3½ oz, add 2 g/½ teaspoon salt.) Mix together.

Using scissors, cut the kombu into thin strips and add to the cucumber. Pour in the soy sauce and mirin and mix well.

Cover the bowl or container, then leave in the fridge for 3–12 hours. Shaking occasionally will speed up curing.

The pickle will keep in the fridge for up to 3 days.

TARTAR SAUCE

Makes 250 ml (1 cup)

JAPANESE TARTAR SAUCE・タルタルソース

- 2 eggs
- 100 g (3½ oz) Japanese mayonnaise
- 1 tablespoon lemon juice
- 1 teaspoon soy sauce
- ½ teaspoon caster (superfine) sugar
- ½ teaspoon Japanese curry powder, or other mild curry powder
- ½ teaspoon ground black pepper
- 2 tablespoons finely diced pickled cucumber (above), seeds removed, or cornichons
- 2 tablespoons baby capers in salt, rinsed
- 1 spring onion (scallion), finely sliced

Bring a saucepan of water to the boil. Add the eggs and boil for 10 minutes. Cool under running water, then peel and roughly chop.

In a bowl, mix together the mayonnaise, lemon juice, soy sauce, sugar, curry powder and pepper. Taste and adjust the seasoning if needed.

Fold in the chopped egg, cucumber, capers and spring onion. The sauce should be chunky, fresh and well balanced.

Use to top the chicken nanban (opposite).

The tartar will keep in the fridge for 1 day.

CLOSING THE LID

On long journeys, an ekiben is a faithful companion, eaten while the scenery slips past the window. But when the lid is closed and the chopsticks are set down, there's often room for something sweet. In Japanese train travel, desserts have long played a quiet supporting role – never large, never excessive, but chosen to round out the dining experience. They're the kind of treats you notice in passing at station kiosks: neatly boxed, carefully wrapped, and designed for travel. These sweets are meant to be enjoyed slowly, often with a cup of tea, as the train gathers speed again.

The drinks and desserts in this chapter are familiar sights across Japan's stations and platforms, and many are deeply tied to their place of origin. Local dairy, regional grains, beans, citrus or tea quietly shape their flavours, offering a final taste of where you are – or where you've just been. Easy to pack, and easy to share, some have been sold for decades and carried home as souvenirs.

Gentle in portion, they leave you content rather than full, carrying with them not just sweetness, but a lingering sense of place as the journey continues.

LANGUE DE CHAT SANDO

Makes about 16

CAT'S TONGUE SANDWICH BISCUITS・ラングドシャサンド

In train stations and airports across Japan, langue de chat – 'cat's tongue' biscuits (cookies) – are a familiar sight in gift shops. The classic form is made of thin, crisp biscuits which sandwich sweetened Hokkaido butter, though variations filled with red bean paste or rum and raisin are also common. This recipe uses rum and raisin, with the raisins soaked in rum the night before, but the raisins can be replaced with cooked adzuki beans (and the rum omitted) if you prefer a more traditional Japanese flavour.

Langue de chat are an excellent way to use up leftover egg whites from other recipes, such as castella (page 232). The baked biscuits freeze well unfilled, making them convenient to prepare in advance.

You can find many langue de chat moulds or stencils online to shape the biscuits neatly. I used an inexpensive 4.5 cm (1¾ in) square one – but any shape works. You can also make them freehand by spreading the batter into even ovals directly onto the baking tray if you prefer.

40 g (1½ oz) butter, at room temperature

40 g (⅓ cup) icing (confectioners') sugar

40 g (1½ oz) egg whites (about 2)

40 g (1½ oz) plain (all-purpose) flour, sifted

RUM AND RAISIN BUTTER FILLING

2 tablespoons raisins

1 tablespoon dark rum

75 g (2¾ oz) butter

2 teaspoons icing (confectioners') sugar, sifted

½ teaspoon vanilla extract

Start on the filling the day before. Mix the raisins and rum in a small container and allow to marinate overnight.

The next day, preheat the oven to 155°C (310°F). Line a baking tray with baking paper or a silicone mat.

In a bowl, whisk together the butter and the icing sugar, using an electric mixer.

Add half the egg whites and whisk on slow speed until combined, then whisk in the flour. (Alternating the addition of wet and dry ingredients makes it easier to combine the ingredients into a smooth batter, without incorporating too much air.)

Whisk in the remaining egg whites.

Place your mould or stencil on the baking tray and spread the batter onto the mould. Use a spatula to smooth the top, then remove the mould. Repeat with the remaining batter.

Transfer to the oven and bake for 15 minutes – the biscuits should be golden brown and crisp. Remove from the oven and leave to cool.

To make the filling, use an electric mixer to beat the butter and icing sugar until pale. Add the vanilla and beat until incorporated. Finely chop the soaked raisins, then fold them through. Any remaining rum can be added as well at this stage.

When the biscuits have cooled, spread ½ teaspoon of the filling on half the biscuits, then sandwich with the remaining halves.

Place in a covered container and chill in the fridge for 20 minutes to firm the butter.

The biscuits are best enjoyed within 2 days. Unfilled biscuits can be frozen in a sealed bag or container for up to 1 month.

SOUFFLÉ CHEESECAKE

スフレチーズケーキ

Makes 9 mini cheesecakes, or 1 large 15 cm (6 in) cheesecake

In Japan, miniature baked goods are everywhere. Train station plazas often fill with long queues for bite-sized croissants, and shops like Mini One and Mignon specialise in selling small pastries by the bag. These mini croissants are designed to be eaten in just two bites – enough to enjoy the flavour without overindulging.

Cakes follow the same philosophy. Soufflé cheesecakes are commonly sold as individual portions in bakeries and department stores, each neatly packaged. Light, airy and gently cheesy, they're easy to carry, and offer a satisfying treat without being heavy – a great companion to an ekiben, something sweet to finish the journey.

- neutral oil, for brushing
- caster (superfine) sugar, for coating
- 100 g (3½ oz) mascarpone, at room temperature
- 100 g (3½ oz) cream cheese, at room temperature
- 40 g (1½ oz) egg yolks (about 3), at room temperature
- 35 g (1¼ oz) caster (superfine) sugar
- 1 teaspoon cornflour (corn starch), sifted
- 2 teaspoons plain (all-purpose) flour, sifted
- 2 teaspoons lemon juice
- 60 g (2 oz) egg whites (about 2), at room temperature
- 1 tablespoon icing (confectioners') sugar

Preheat the oven to 180°C (350°F).

Place nine small round or oval moulds, about 3 cm (1¼ in) deep and 10–12 cm (4–4¾ in) in diameter, on a lined baking tray. Brush the interior with oil, then line the sides with baking paper, using a little more oil to help it adhere if the paper doesn't sit well. Oil the inside of the paper as well, then coat the walls with caster sugar.

Using an electric mixer fitted with the paddle attachment, mix together the mascarpone and cream cheese until well combined. Mix in the egg yolks, a third at a time, until incorporated.

Then add, in order, 10 g (¼ oz) of the caster sugar, the cornflour, the plain flour, and finally the lemon juice, mixing after each addition until fully incorporated.

In a clean bowl, whisk the egg whites until soft peaks form. Slowly add the remaining 25 g (1 oz) of caster sugar and continue to whisk until the sugar dissolves and the mixture holds a medium peak.

Fold the egg white mixture through the egg yolk mixture.

Evenly divide the mixture between the moulds, about 35 g (1¼ oz) per mould. Using a skewer, gently draw figure eights in the batter to evenly distribute it in each mould.

Bake for 10 minutes, then turn the oven down to 110°C (230°F) and bake for a further 30 minutes.

Remove from the oven and allow to cool in the moulds, to room temperature, before turning them out and removing the baking paper.

Place in a container and chill in the fridge for 1–2 hours.

Sprinkle with the icing sugar and serve, or keep in the fridge for up to 3 days.

NAMA CHOCO

生チョコ

Makes about 50 squares

Nama choco is a soft, ganache-style chocolate most closely associated with Hokkaido, popularised by the confectioner ROYCE. It is a deliberately simple sweet, designed to showcase the quality of its ingredients rather than technique or decoration.

Hokkaido is celebrated for its dairy as much as its seafood, and nama choco makes full use of that reputation. Cream and butter lend a gentle richness to the chocolate, creating a texture that is smooth, cool and almost melting, without heaviness. Served chilled and dusted lightly with cocoa, it feels understated yet carefully considered.

200 g (7 oz) high-quality milk or dark chocolate (at least 70% cocoa solids)
60 ml (¼ cup) pure cream
15 g (½ oz) butter
2 tablespoons unsweetened cocoa powder

Line a 15 cm (6 in) baking tray with plastic wrap, making sure it's smooth on the bottom, with no wrinkles.

Place the chocolate in a microwave-safe bowl. (If using a block of chocolate, cut it into small pieces first.) Microwave in 30-second intervals, mixing each time, until the chocolate is fully melted.

In a saucepan, bring the cream to a simmer. Turn the heat off, add the chocolate and mix until well combined. Add the butter, mixing until combined.

Pour into the baking tray, smoothing the top. Gently drop the tray onto a tea towel to release any trapped air pockets.

Place in the fridge and chill for at least 2 hours (or overnight).

When the chocolate has hardened, remove from the baking tray. You may need to dip the base of the tray in hot water to release the chocolate. Using a hot knife, cut into 2 cm (¾ in) squares. Dust with the cocoa powder and serve.

The nama choco can be refrigerated for up to 5 days, or frozen for up to 1 month.

NOTE //

For a tea variation, substitute the dark chocolate with white chocolate and add a tablespoon of finely sifted tea powder, such as matcha. Finish with an extra dusting of tea powder in place of cocoa for a clean, aromatic finish.

OSHIRUKO

Serves 4

ADZUKI BEAN SOUP WITH MOCHI・お汁粉

In Kansai, western Japan, zenzai is a soupy dessert with chunky beans, while oshiruko is soupy with a smooth paste; conversely, in the Kanto region in eastern Japan, oshiruko is the general term for any soupy red bean soup (smooth or chunky), and zenzai refers to a drier version with a chunky paste, often served with toasted mochi. It gets confusing.

What we're making is a chunky red bean 'soup' topped with shiratama, or chewy mochi. It's a great drink, dessert and hand-warmer on cold winter days.

- 100 g (3½ oz) dried adzuki (red beans)
- 80 g (⅓ cup) caster (superfine) sugar
- ½ teaspoon salt
- 4 pieces dried mochi or 8 homemade shiratama balls (see below)

SHIRATAMA

- 100 g (3½ oz) shiratamako rice flour (or mochi flour or glutinous rice flour)
- 1 teaspoon icing (confectioners') sugar

If making the shiratama, bring a large saucepan of water to the boil over high heat, and fill a large bowl with iced water.

In a mixing bowl, combine the rice flour and icing sugar. Slowly stir in 100 ml (3½ fl oz) water until it comes together as a dough; you may not need all the water.

Shape the dough into balls about 2 cm (¾ in) in diameter; you should end up with 12. Carefully place the balls into the boiling water and cook for about 5 minutes, until they begin to float. Remove using a slotted spoon and immediately transfer to the iced water. Keep in iced water until required.

To prepare the soup, place the dried beans in a large saucepan and cover with cold water. Bring to the boil over medium-high heat, then leave to boil for 15 minutes, skimming off any scum that appears on the surface.

Drain the beans and cover with 600 ml (20½ fl oz) fresh cold water. Bring back to the boil, then reduce the heat and simmer for a further 45 minutes. Skim regularly during this time, stirring and topping up the water if required. The beans are done when they crush easily.

When the beans are soft, turn the heat to medium-low and add the sugar, stirring well to incorporate and dissolve the sugar.

Continue cooking for 15–20 minutes, stirring regularly so the mixture doesn't burn on the bottom, and adding water if needed to stop it getting too thick.

Stir in the salt, then adjust the thickness by adding more water if necessary. Keep warm.

If using store-bought dried mochi, place under an oven grill (broiler) preheated to high until browned and puffed, but not burnt; this should only take a minute or two. (There is no need to grill if you are using homemade shiratama.)

Place the red beans in a bowl and top with the mochi or shiratama. Serve hot.

ZUNDA SHAKE

ずんだシェイク

Serves 2

Tohoku, in northern Japan, is known for its unusually sweet edamame. Unlike the starchy or strongly savoury soybeans used in cooking, these beans have a gentle sweetness, closer to sweetcorn, with a clean, green aroma. This quality makes them well suited to desserts.

Zunda is the name given to edamame that has been lightly cooked, mashed and sweetened into a vivid green paste. Its flavour is fresh and delicate rather than heavy, which is why it pairs so well with dairy. Blended into ice cream or milkshakes, zunda cuts through the richness of milk and cream while adding a uniquely Japanese sweetness.

150 g (5½ oz) edamame
150 ml (5 fl oz) milk
1 tablespoon condensed milk
¼ teaspoon salt
150 g (5½ oz) ice cream (vanilla or matcha)

Blanch the edamame in a saucepan of boiling water for 5 minutes, then refresh in iced water.

Remove the pods from the edamame. You should end up with about 75 g (2¾ oz) edamame beans.

Freeze the edamame for 15–20 minutes, to harden the beans so they blend more easily.

Using a blender or food processor, blend the edamame with the milk, condensed milk and salt.

Add the ice cream and pulse a couple of times until just incorporated.

Pour into glasses and enjoy straight away, as you would at the train station.

AKAFUKU MOCHI

Makes 10

赤福餅

Akafuku mochi is a regional sweet from Ise, in Mie Prefecture, closely tied to place and ritual. Its distinctive form is marked by three gentle ridges, traditionally shaped by hand in the red bean paste to evoke the flowing waters of the Isuzu River. This river runs beside Ise Jingu, Japan's most sacred Shinto shrine, and the design connects the sweet directly to the landscape and its spiritual significance.

Unlike most mochi, where the rice cake wraps the filling, akafuku encloses a soft white mochi within a layer of koshi-an (smooth red bean paste). The result is a tender contrast between the chewy rice cake and the fine-textured bean paste. While the finger-pressed ridges are not essential, they give the mochi a sense of intention and care, reinforcing its identity as something made by hand, rather than assembled.

70 g (2½ oz) shiratamako rice flour (or mochi flour or glutinous rice flour)

30 g (1 oz) caster (superfine) sugar

90 ml (3 fl oz) room-temperature water

2 tablespoons potato starch

SMOOTH RED BEAN PASTE

200 g (7 oz) dried adzuki (red beans)

180 g (6½ oz) caster (superfine) sugar

½ teaspoon salt

To make the red bean paste, place the red beans in a large saucepan and cover with cold water. Bring to a boil and boil over medium-high heat for 15 minutes. Skim off any scum that appears on the surface of the water.

Drain and rinse the beans, then cover with 600 ml (20½ fl oz) fresh cold water. Bring back to the boil, then reduce the heat and simmer for a further 45 minutes. Skim regularly during this time, stirring and topping up the water if required. The beans are done when they crush easily.

When the beans are soft, mash them using a potato masher, then blend in a blender.

Place a fine-mesh sieve over a bowl. Working in batches, press the contents of the blender through the sieve, discarding what's left over in the sieve.

Place a sheet of muslin over a clean sieve and pour the blended red bean paste mixture into the muslin. Firmly gather up the corners of the cloth and squeeze thoroughly to extract any excess water. Rinse the outside of the cloth with water to rinse off the excess starch from the beans. Set aside.

Add the sugar, salt and 50 ml (1¾ fl oz) water to a large saucepan and heat to dissolve the sugar and salt, stirring regularly. Add the cooked beans and mix for 5 minutes, until the consistency has thickened, like play dough, and comes easily off the side of the pan. The mixture may splatter, so be careful. Test if it's done by pressing the cooled dough with your fingers; it should be firm but pliable, without cracking.

Spread the red bean paste mixture on a heatproof tray, press plastic wrap onto the surface and allow to cool to room temperature. You'll have more red bean paste than you need for this recipe; any leftovers can be used to make other mochi, such as kusamochi (page 107).

To make the akafuku mochi, place the rice flour and sugar in a microwave-safe bowl. Whisk to combine, then gradually whisk in the water until smooth. Cover with plastic wrap and microwave at 500W for 2 minutes. Mix with a spatula, cover again and microwave for a further 1 minute.

Dust a work surface with potato starch. Transfer the mochi to the work surface, divide into 10 pieces and roll into smooth balls.

Take 250 g (9 oz) of the red bean paste and divide into 10 pieces. Place one portion on a square of plastic wrap, then flatten into a 5 mm (¼ in) disc. Place a mochi ball in the centre and wrap to enclose the mochi. Wrap your fingers around the top of the mochi to recreate the distinctive ridges. Repeat with the remaining red bean paste and mochi balls.

Keep in the plastic wrap until ready to serve. They are best consumed the same day, but will last at room temperature for up to 2 days.

CASTELLA

HONEY SPONGE CAKE・カステラ

Makes an 18 cm (7 in) square cake; serves 16

Castella embodies the ideals of Japanese baking: restraint, precision and quiet skill. It is not a cake that demands attention; instead, it conveys refinement through consistency and care.

Arrive in Nagasaki and castella is everywhere. Bakery windows display loaves with sharp edges and evenly burnished tops, a visual shorthand for experience rather than novelty. Fukusaya, which maintains a branch inside Nagasaki Station, has been making castella since 1624, and that longevity is evident in every detail – from the uniform crumb to the immaculate finish.

The texture of this cake is light yet composed. Airy, but not fragile like chiffon, castella feels built to travel. Traditionally packed in wooden boxes, it has long been made with gifting in mind, carried home for friends and family or sent further afield as a taste of Nagasaki.

This recipe is a straightforward version that allows the honeyed flavour to come through clearly, finished with coarse sugar at the base for small bursts of crunch – just as you'd find in a classic Fukusaya-style castella.

The cake needs to rest in the fridge for 3 days before serving, to reabsorb the steam from the oven for a moist result, and for the honey flavour to mature and fully permeate the cake.

- 6 egg yolks (about 100 g/3½ oz in total)
- 150 g (5½ oz) caster (superfine) sugar
- 30 ml (1 fl oz) neutral oil
- 50 g (1¾ oz) honey
- 40 ml (1¼ fl oz) mirin
- 40 ml (1¼ fl oz) milk
- 5 egg whites (about 175 g/6 oz in total)
- 150 g (1 cup) bread flour
- 2 tablespoons coarse sugar or pearl sugar

Preheat the oven to 180°C (350°F). Line an 18 cm (7 in) square cake tin with baking paper.

Using an electric mixer, whisk the egg yolks with half the caster sugar for about 5 minutes, until very pale. Add the oil in a thin stream, whisking constantly until incorporated, as if making a mayonnaise.

In a microwave-safe container, combine the honey, mirin and milk. Microwave for 15 seconds. Mix until the honey is incorporated, then mix gently into the egg yolk mixture.

Using a clean electric mixer, whisk the egg whites into soft peaks. Add the remaining caster sugar, one-third at a time, until it comes to a medium peak.

Whisk the egg white mixture into the egg yolk mixture, one-third at a time. Sift in the flour and whisk to combine. Continue whisking gently for a further minute or so, until the mixture becomes the consistency of pouring cream.

Sprinkle the coarse sugar in the bottom of the cake tin and gently pour the batter on top. Use a wooden skewer to make zigzag motions through the batter to puncture any large air bubbles.

Bake for 10 minutes, then reduce the oven temperature to 150°C (300°F). Bake for a further 35–40 minutes, until a skewer comes out clean.

Remove the tin from the oven, carefully drop the tin lightly on a tea towel to release the steam, then remove the cake from the tin.

Wrap lightly in plastic wrap and leave face down in the fridge for 3 days to set. It will then keep for up to 5 days in an airtight container.

To serve, cut in half, then cut each half into eight slices.

BAUMKUCHEN

バームクーヘン

Makes an 18 cm (7 in) square cake; serves 16

Baumkuchen is a cake of German origin that has found an enduring home in Japan. Today it is one of the most recognisable sweets in stations and depachika (luxury department store food halls), often boxed with the same care and formality as a fine gift.

Its name means 'tree cake', a reference to both its construction and its appearance. Traditionally, the batter is ladled on in thin layers, smoothed, then baked one layer at a time on a rotating spit. Each layer browns before the next is added – and when the cake is sliced, the interior reveals rings like those of a tree trunk. The process is slow and exacting, demanding patience and attention, which is part of the cake's appeal.

Most home kitchens, however, lack a rotisserie. This version adapts the technique for a standard oven, building the cake layer by layer by repeatedly returning it to the heat and spreading fresh batter on top. It remains a time-intensive process, but one that rewards care with a cake unlike any other – dense yet tender, evenly baked and quietly impressive.

The recipe uses eight eggs in total. Make sure they are at room temperature before you begin; cold eggs can cause the batter to split and compromise the texture.

- 8 eggs, at room temperature
- 40 g (1½ oz) almond flour
- 2 teaspoons icing (confectioners') sugar
- 225 g (8 oz) unsalted butter, at room temperature
- 120 g (4½ oz) honey
- ½ teaspoon salt
- ½ teaspoon vanilla extract
- 35 ml (1¼ fl oz) dark rum
- 115 g (4 oz) caster (superfine) sugar
- 135 g (4¾ oz) cake flour
- 110 g (4 oz) cornflour (corn starch)
- 1 teaspoon baking powder

WHITE CHOCOLATE GLAZE

- 80 g (2¾ oz) white chocolate
- 1 tablespoon neutral oil

Separate the egg yolks from the egg whites, reserving two of the egg whites for the cake batter, and six egg whites for the meringue.

Preheat the oven grill (broiler) to high.

Grease an 18 cm square cake tin thoroughly with oil. Line the bottom with baking paper and dust the sides with flour.

Sift the almond flour and icing sugar into the bowl of a stand mixer with either the paddle or whisk attachment fitted. Using the two reserved egg whites (about 70 g/2½ oz), mix in 1 tablespoon of the egg white at a time until well combined.

With the paddle attachment, mix in the butter until incorporated and pale in colour.

Add the honey and salt and mix until well combined.

One at a time, add the eight egg yolks, incorporating each yolk well before adding the next. Mix in the vanilla and rum.

In a separate bowl, whisk the sugar with the remaining six egg whites (about 210 g/7½ oz) until medium-stiff peaks form.

Add one-third of the meringue to the egg yolk mixture and fold in with a spatula. Repeat with the remaining meringue, one-third at a time.

Sift in the cake flour, cornflour and the baking powder and gently incorporate with the spatula.

Pour about 2 heaped tablespoons (or one ice-cream scoop) of the batter into the prepared cake tin. Spread it out evenly using an offset spatula, adding more batter if necessary. Place under the grill and cook for 4–5 minutes, until lightly browned.

Remove from the grill and place on a damp cloth to cool the bottom of the cake tin. Add another layer of the batter and cook again for 4–5 minutes.

Repeat until all the batter is used. You should end up with 10–12 layers.

Once the last layer is browned, allow to cool on the tray, then use a palette knife to release the cake from the sides of the tray.

Turn the cooled cake out onto a flat tray.

To make the white chocolate glaze, melt the chocolate in the microwave (in 30 second intervals), then fold in the oil, being careful not to incorporate any bubbles. Pour over the cake, smoothing with a palette knife. Allow the chocolate to harden for about 15 minutes, then cut off the sides (as a snack for your hard work).

Cut the cake into 4.5 cm (1¾ in) squares, to give you 16 portions. The cake will keep in the fridge in an airtight container for up to 5 days.

GLOSSARY

Abura-age (油揚げ) are pockets of fried tofu that can be used to add texture and flavour to dishes, as they are excellent at absorbing flavour. You'll find them in the freezer section of Asian grocery stores.

Benishoga (紅生姜) is a variation of pickled ginger that's bright pink and cut into small shards. The pink colour traditionally comes from umeboshi pickling liquid, but in more recent times from food colouring.

Chicken stock powder (鶏ガラスープ) is the distinctive flavour in many Chinese-Japanese dishes and adds a concentrated burst of umami. You can omit this, but some of the dish's character will be lost. Chicken stock powder can be substituted with instant dashi powder.

Daikon (大根) is a long, white Japanese radish. It's very versatile and can be used raw, pickled or braised. Raw grated or shredded daikon (known as daikon oroshi) is a very common palate cleanser in izakayas. With a dash of ponzu, daikon oroshi is a great side for grilled dishes.

Demi-glace (デミグラスソース) is a reduced beef or veal stock popular in yoshoku (洋食) – Western cuisine adapted to Japanese tastes. You can make your own demi-glace by slowly reducing beef or veal stock to about one-quarter of its original volume. If using store bought, use a salt-reduced stock, as a regular stock will end up extremely salty.

Doubanjiang, also known as **tobanjan** (豆板醤), is a chilli sauce made from broad beans that's most famous as the flavouring for mapo tofu. It has a salty, savoury, spicy flavour that's the basis for many Korean, Sichuan and Chinese-Japanese dishes.

Hanpen (はんぺん) is a fluffy textured, white fish paste with yama imo (Japanese mountain yam) and egg whites. It's blended and used as the base for dumplings, or cut up and added to stews and soups.

Hijiki (ひじき) is a frilly Japanese seaweed, normally found dried in-store. It's cooked by rehydrating, then quickly stir-frying. The preparation technique is unique as most other seaweeds are simply rehydrated. It has a mild flavour and soft texture.

Kani miso (蟹味噌) is the guts of the crab. It doesn't sound very appealing, but it has a wonderful, rich crab flavour. If you pick your own crab, you can find it in the shell (it's the brown part inside the head), or you can find it in the frozen section of Asian grocery stores.

Kizami nori (刻み海苔) is simply nori that's been shredded. It's usually used as a topping for rice.

Joshinko (上新粉) is a fine flour made from non-glutinous rice. It's firmer, less sticky and chewier than glutinous rice flour, making it ideal for mochi as it's easier to work with.

Mayonnaise (マヨネーズ) in this book is Japanese mayo. It is eggier than Western mayonnaise, with the addition of MSG giving it a distinctive flavour. Most Japanese varieties have a similar flavour profile based on the popular brand Kewpie.

Mentaiko (明太子) is the salted, preserved roe of the Alaskan pollock fish. Usually found frozen outside Japan, mentaiko has a clean, briny fish flavour with the added kick of chilli. **Tarako** (たらこ) is the non-spicy version.

Mirin (みりん) is a type of rice wine made from glutinous rice that adds sweetness and umami to dishes. Real mirin or hon mirin should contain no added sugar, with the sweetness coming from the natural fermentation of glutinous rice with koji; real mirin is expensive and difficult to find. Most store-bought mirin is a blend of real mirin (本みりん) and glucose syrup. This is fine to use in these recipes.

Miso (味噌) is a fermented paste containing soy beans and rice koji (rice inoculated with spores to aid fermentation). Light-coloured miso has a sweeter, lighter flavour, whereas dark miso is fermented longer and has a richer, almost soy sauce–like flavour. Each region has their own favoured type, such as Sendai with its reddish miso, and Nagoya, with hatcho miso.

Nori (のり/海苔) are dried seaweed sheets commonly used to wrap sushi and onigiri. Quality nori is crisp, not chewy, and holds its structure well, rather than falling apart. Most supermarkets now stock seaweed sheets, but if not, check the snack aisle in Asian grocery stores. These seaweeds can be used as toppings, but are usually quite salty, so be careful. They are also often small, which prevents them being used for sushi.

Panko (パン粉) are Japanese breadcrumbs that come in large shards, resulting in a shatteringly crisp crust on fried products. The dried version is available in most supermarkets. Fresh panko can be hard to find, but is sometimes stocked in the frozen section of Asian grocers. Fresh panko has larger shards that work well with firm ingredients like pork steaks (as in tonkatsu), whereas finer breadcrumbs are good for croquettes or softer fillings, as they easily coat the entire surface, sealing the moisture inside.

Potato starch (片栗粉) is used in a variety of applications, from thickening soups and sauces to giving fried food a very crisp coating.

Rice (米) – Every grain of rice is valuable, a lesson taught to every Japanese person from a very young age. There are many different types of Japanese rice, with varying grades of stickiness depending on whether it's table rice or sushi rice. Ask your Japanese grocer which rice is best for your purpose; rice from Niigata, Aomori, Akita or Hokkaido are good options.

Rice vinegar (米酢) has a mild tartness and sweetness that works for any Japanese salad dressing and as a vinegar base for pickling. It is much less astringent than Western vinegar, so substitute with caution.

Roasted sesame seeds (いりごま) are used either whole or crushed, and are a great way to add texture to sashimi, rice and salads. They can also come in a variety of flavours such as ume (pickled plum) or wasabi.

Roasted sesame seed oil (ごま油) adds a pleasant nutty characteristic to many dishes. It comes in a variety of grades, from cheap to expensive. The inexpensive versions are fine, but the higher-quality ones will add an extra dimension to your cooking.

Sake (酒 or 料理酒) is in fact a general term for all alcohol – wine and spirits included. In this book we use it to refer to cooking sake. Sake is alcohol made from rice and koji, and can add a floral and light flavour to dishes. For cooking, only use cooking sake (ryori shu). It has a simple, rounded flavour that pairs well with all food. Drinking sake can sometimes have unique flavours and characteristics that may not work well in cooking.

Sansho (山椒) is the berry of the Japanese prickly ash tree. It's most often sold in dried, powdered form. It has a unique, numbing, citrus flavour. A little Sichuan peppercorn can be used as a substitute, but it won't have the citrus element.

Shio koji (塩麹) is a versatile seasoning made from koji (rice that's been inoculated with *Aspergillus oryzae*), water and salt. Koji is the base for many Japanese products such as soy sauce and miso, and shio koji is sold in liquid or paste form. Its enzymes break down proteins and starches, adding a savoury depth, slight sweetness and improved texture.

Shio kombu (塩昆布) are strands of kombu seaweed, usually an inch long, lightly covered in salt. It's usually mixed with rice. It can be cooked with the rice, and the kombu flavour will evenly permeate the rice, or it can be added after cooking for pops of flavour.

Shiratamako (白玉粉)is a glutinous rice flour used for making mochi and other Japanese desserts. You'll often find it comes in large pieces, and it's worthwhile blending it to make it easier to incorporate into doughs. Otherwise, mix it in the recipes with warm liquid to dissolve.

Shiso (しそ), also known as perilla leaf, comes in two varieties: a green variety called oba, and a purple variety called akajiso. The leaves have a distinct, herbaceous flavour, as do the delicate, tiny purple flowers (穂紫蘇), which are typically eaten with sashimi. Shiso can be found fresh in the refrigerated section of Asian fruit and vegetable stores.

Soy sauce in these recipes is koikuchi shoyu (濃口醤油) or dark soy sauce. It has a pleasant soy flavour and is moderately salty. Please use a low-sodium koikuchi shoyu if you can find it, as this allows you to adjust the soy flavour and salt to your liking.

Umeboshi (梅干し) are pickled Japanese plums that can add a wonderful fruity sweetness and acidity to dishes. The colour and flavour comes from pickling with red shiso leaves. They're great mashed into a salad dressing or as a salty, sour accent to many dishes. Umeboshi are also commonly eaten on their own in the centre of a bowl of rice as a simple meal.

Usukuchi shoyu (薄口醤油) or light soy is lighter in colour than regular soy sauce, but don't let that deceive you – it's actually a little saltier. It does have a lighter soy flavouring, though. Use it when you want a milder soy taste or to keep a lighter colour in sauces and soups.

Yomogi (よもぎ) – also known as mugwort – is a leafy green used to add flavour to sweets. It has a grassy, slightly bitter flavour. It's most often found outside Japan in powder form.

Zarame (ざらめ) is a light brown sugar with large, coarse grains. It's less sweet than regular sugar and has a more complex flavour that works well in braises and sauces for meat. Substitute with demerara sugar if unavailable.

みりん
醤油
酒

INDEX

A

B

C

D

E

F

G

H

I

J

K

L

M

N

O

P

Q

R

S

T

U

V

W

Z

ACKNOWLEDGEMENTS

Writing this book, like a train journey, has been one of discovery and fortunate meetings.

My thanks to the ekiben makers, collectors, writers and railway enthusiasts who shared their time, knowledge and memories so freely. Their dedication to preserving regional food and rail culture made this book possible.

I am especially grateful to Kenichi Fukuoka and the invaluable archive of the ekibenmuseum.org; Hashima Tomoyuki, whose reflections on rail travel and collecting offered a rare glimpse into a disappearing world; and Mai Nakamura from JR Cross, who shared insights from the perspective of an ekiben manufacturer.

Thank you to my photographer in Japan, Masaharu Okuda, who met me on a rainy Tokyo day to collect dozens of ekiben; and to my photographer in Australia, Daniel Herrmann-Zoll, and food stylist, Meryl Batlle. Archive photography was kindly provided by The Railway Museum in Saitama.

Thank you also to the team at Smith Street Books for their support, guidance and belief in this project from the very beginning. A special thank you to Michelle Mackintosh for designing and illustrating the book, to Katri Hilden for editing it and to Mifumi Obata for fact-checking.

Finally, thank you to Amanda, who came on this journey with me and endured many detours, station stops and recipe trials along the way.

Like the journeys that inspired it, this book was shaped as much by the people encountered along the route as the destination itself.

ABOUT THE AUTHOR

A chef by training, Brendan Liew has worked both internationally and locally – from stints at restaurants including Kadeau in Copenhagen and Benu in San Francisco, to the three-Michelin-starred Nihonryori Ryugin in Tokyo and Hong Kong. He studied the craft of ramen making in Osaka before settling on specialising in kappo and modern kaiseki cuisine. Locally in Melbourne, Brendan has worked at revered Edomae sushi restaurant Minamishima, Warabi and Supernormal.

He has authored 3 cookbooks, *A Day in Tokyo*, *Tokyo Up Late* and *Konbini*, with *Tokyo Up Late* named in *The New York Times*' 'The Best Cookbooks of 2022.'

Smith Street Books

Published in 2026 by Smith Street Books
Naarm (Melbourne) | Australia
smithstreetbooks.com

Distributed outside of ANZ, North & Latin America
by Thames & Hudson Ltd., 6–24 Britannia Street,
London, WC1X 9JD
thamesandhudson.com

EU Authorised Representative: Interart S.A.R.L.
19 rue Charles Auray, 93500 Pantin, Paris, France
productsafety@thameshudson.co.uk;
www.interart.fr

ISBN: 978-1-9235-0338-0

Smith Street Books respectfully acknowledges the Wurundjeri People of the Kulin Nation, who are the Traditional Owners of the land on which we work, and we pay our respects to their Elders past and present.

Publisher: Megan Cuthbert
Project editor: Elena Callcott
Editor: Katri Hilden
Designer and illustrator: Michelle Mackintosh
Ekiben photography: Masaharu Okuda
Recipe photography: Daniel Herrmann-Zoll
Recipe food stylist: Meryl Batlle
Food preparation: Brendan Liew & Caroline Griffiths
Typesetting & pre-press: Megan Ellis
English proofread: Pamela Dunne
Japanese proofread and fact-checking: Mifumi Obata
Indexer: Max McMaster
Production manager: Aisling Coughlan

Printed & bound in China by C&C Offset Printing Co., Ltd.

Book 488
10 9 8 7 6 5 4 3 2 1

MIX
Paper | Supporting responsible forestry
FSC www.fsc.org FSC® C008047